Finding Love After a Breakup

Crack the Code of Modern Dating, Build Unshakeable Confidence, and Find Your Perfect Match

Tristan Brody

Acknowledgements

This book stands as a testament to the power of friendship and the unwavering support that carried me through a challenging chapter of my life.

To each and every one of you who stood by my side, lending an ear, offering a shoulder, and sharing in both my tears and my triumphs, thank you. Your presence has been a gift beyond measure, and this book would not exist without your love and encouragement.

As I embark on this new chapter of my life, your friendship serves as a constant reminder that I am never alone. I am blessed to have you as a part of my story, and I am grateful beyond words.

To my two faithful companions Oliver & Leo, who fill my days with love and laughter, this book is dedicated to you.

In the depths of loneliness and heartache, you were there, by my side, with your unwavering presence and unconditional affection.

Through the ups and downs of life's journey, you brought joy to my soul, chasing away the shadows of solitude.

With each gentle purr, you reminded me of the beauty in simple moments, and the power of a loving bond.

You taught me the true meaning of loyalty and devotion, and through your unwavering companionship, you showed me that love knows no bounds.

Tristan

Introduction

If you find yourself reading this book, chances are you're facing the challenge of finding love again after the conclusion of a significant long-term relationship or divorce.

Like me, you may be venturing back out into the dating world, and you've discovered that the landscape has shifted, and the rules have changed.

After twenty years, my partner decided it was time for a divorce. If you've read my first book, *Finding Yourself After a Breakup for Men – Recovering from Heartbreak at the End of a Long-term Relationship*, then you are well aware of the story. If not, don't worry.

I arrived home to an empty house and a letter on the kitchen bench. It was a letter that no one ever wants to receive from the person that they have shared so much of their life with, my partner had decided to end it all.

The heartbreak following the end of a twenty-year-long relationship is a pain that I would never wish on anybody.

Throughout the marriage, I developed a sense of comfort, of belonging. I found fulfilment in my work, but it was the moments of returning home to my family that truly brought me joy. Suddenly, all that had been uprooted. How could this happen?

As I grappled with the conclusion of my marriage, I discovered solace and a sense of belonging among others who were navigating similar heartbreaks. I met people who had seen their 40, 50-year long marriages end. Others I met were fresh from fairly short but still deeply intimate relationships.

I discovered that both men and women were experiencing a hard time getting past their failed relationship and finding someone else to love. Suddenly, people like you and I who had not been in the dating scene for years were thrust back into a dating landscape they are unfamiliar with. Where do they begin? How would they even go about it?

As I asked myself these questions, I realized that I could leverage my knowledge from my previous book to write a guide for people in similar situations to help them find love once more.

Most people that I met would simply wish for someone to hold them and remind them that they are loveable, that they are worthy, and that they deserve great things.

And the fact that you are holding this book means that you are one of those people. You may be struggling to get back to a dating scene, which is vastly different from what you knew the last time you were here. Perhaps you are wondering:

Will I ever find love again?

Will I ever get over the pain of heartbreak from my failed relationship/marriage?

Do I have what it takes to date in the modern world?

There is nothing quite as devastating as learning that a relationship you had banked so much hope on could end so abruptly. And, I know that you may be experiencing a mixture of sorrow, shame, guilt, and loneliness, but the fact that you have this book means that you want to get over these feelings and find love again.

And worry not, this book will guide you to finding the one for you.

In this book, you will come to understand that:

You are not alone in trying to find love after a divorce or failed long-term relationship. According to statistics, more than 70% of divorcees often end up remarrying at some point in their life, while over 80% of people who had been cohabiting get into another relationship.

No matter how devastating the heartbreak was, you will get over it and fall in love with someone else again if that is what you choose to do, or simply, enjoy dating again.

More specifically, in the chapters to follow, we will explore different topics related to recovering from heartbreak such as:

- How to process emotions after a breakup to heal

- Rebuilding your confidence so that you get back into dating without any fear

- How to navigate dating in the modern world, especially the world of online dating

- How to become vulnerable and learn to trust again

- And so much more!

I believe that having been down this path, my story will provide an element of relatability to the advice I give. You can be sure that what you read in this book will be more than theories.

They will be things that I learned as I went through my heartbreak which can then help you get over yours.

So, without any more chit-chat, how about we get down to business and begin working on finding love!

Table of Contents

Acknowledgements **2**

Introduction **4**

Chapter 1: Healing and Reflection **13**

Processing Your Emotions and Finding Closure . 15

Reflections After a Breakup for Growth Opportunities 22

Chapter 2: Building Unshakeable Confidence **32**

Boosting Self-Esteem and Embracing Self-Love . 33

Stepping into Your Authentic Self 46

Chapter 3: Navigating the World of Online Dating **64**

Finding The Best App for You 65

Crafting an Appealing and Genuine Online Dating Profile 71

Chapter 4: Effective Communication and Boundaries 84

How to Build Effective Communication Skills in Dating 85

Establishing and Maintaining Boundaries in New Relationships 92

Chapter 5: Embracing Vulnerability and Trust 103

Embracing Vulnerability as a Strength in Dating 104

How To Build Vulnerability 107

Building Trust in Yourself and Others After a Breakup 109

Chapter 6: Overcoming Dating Anxiety 115

Managing Anxiety and Fears Associated with Dating 116

Readiness, Rejection, and Retreating into Yourself 129

Chapter 7: Red Flags and Healthy Relationship Dynamics 132

Recognizing Warning Signs and Red Flags in Potential Partners 134

Nurturing Healthy Relationship Dynamics Based on Respect and Compatibility 141

Chapter 8: Exploring Diverse Relationships and Orientations 149

Navigating Dating as a Member of the LGBTQ+ Community 154

Chapter 9: Developing Intimacy and Connection 162

Rediscovering Intimacy and Establishing Emotional Connections 162

Nurturing Physical and Emotional Intimacy in New Relationships 170

Chapter 10: Creating a Lasting Connection 178

Recognizing Compatibility and Shared Values ..178

Building a Strong Foundation for a Long-term, Fulfilling Relationship 186

Conclusion 190

Before you go 194

Endnotes 195

Chapter 1: Healing and Reflection

One overcast Tuesday morning several months ago, on my way to work, I bumped into an old friend. Let's call him Alfie. Alfie and I had previously worked together and while we hadn't exactly been particularly close, familiarity hung in the air.

Alfie had always been a bubbly and lively man for those many years we worked together, and he seemed to have retained much of his spark that day when we met. As we did some catching up however, Alfie confided in me.

"It's been close to two years, Tristan, and I am no closer to healing now than I was when we broke up. I really want to date again, to meet new people, and meet the love of my life, but the past keeps holding me back and I don't know what to do."

Alfie's story is one that many of you reading this book may relate to. After the end of a long-term relationship, you feel lost, and hurt; you weep for what could have been from your old relationship. Yet, making the next step can be extremely hard.

Alfie and I exchanged numbers and over the next few weeks, we met up and talked a couple of times. I explained to Alfie that I believe closure is more than just getting answers or apologies; instead, it involves accepting that even though things didn't go as planned or hoped for – life moves forward nonetheless!

He hadn't yet started dating, but he was no longer fearful of the idea. He had started going out and meeting people, and simply being open to the idea that he may just meet someone special.

Just like Alfie, you might relate to a situation where dating was off the table for a year or more after your divorce. The idea of meeting new people or sharing your life with someone might have seemed daunting, and the very thought of sleeping beside another person felt unimaginable.

Often, we construct our own mental barriers following heartbreak, and until we heal, these barriers can hinder our dating journey.

So, how do you initiate the healing process?

Processing Your Emotions and Finding Closure

One of the biggest myths perpetuated by our society and one that, unfortunately, many people gleefully buy into is evading the pain. You've probably all heard the saying 'To get over someone, you should get under someone'.

Maybe this saying was said in jest, but you and I both know just how many people often try to get over heartbreak by having a rebound relationship.

I'm not going to go into any ethical arguments about rebounds, it's your life and your choices. The fact is though, if you do wish to completely get over your heartbreak and heal, then you will need to face your feelings head on.

Escapism, or trying to dull the pain you feel through a rebound is <u>not how to process emotions</u>[i]. It may provide some short-term physical contact, but ultimately you need time to process what has happened so you can to try to prevent it in future relationships.

Divorce triggers a wide range of emotions, from sadness and anger to confusion and possibly even relief. It's crucial to acknowledge and accept all of these feelings as a normal part of the process.

By giving yourself permission to feel, you're taking the *first step toward emotional healing.*

Allow Yourself to Sit with The Pain

As painful as it is, there is no escaping the reality that getting over someone you once loved involves allowing yourself to feel the hurt.

Just like any loss, divorce warrants a period of mourning. Allow yourself to grieve the end of your marriage and the dreams you once shared with your partner. It's okay to feel sad, frustrated, or even lost during this phase. Grieving is a way of honoring what was, and it will eventually lead you to a place of acceptance.

I know this advice goes against what mainstream media or articles may have repeatedly told you, but failing to deal with the pain is like kicking an empty can down the road ahead of you.

Sure, you eliminate the nuisance of having a can in your way, but it is only momentary. You will inevitably walk a bit further down the road and the can will once again be blocking your path. It is simply postponing the inevitable.

If you fail to create time to hurt after a breakup, that time will create itself, and trust me, when the body decides that it wants to deal with the pain, you will have no control.

Like me, you may be there, in the middle of a meeting with a client, and unexpectedly, a burst of pain explodes from your chest. Suddenly you can't stop thinking about what went wrong with your ex and the tears start to flow.

So, go through the feelings of rejection and pain. Feel sad and angry and be in denial too. Turn up your stereo and listen to sad music and if the music is not sad enough, sit up and sob all night – but most of all <u>allow yourself to feel it</u>[ii]!

Heck, from time to time, if you feel like screaming, find somewhere quiet and private, and scream it all out.

If you need to and if possible, take time off work to nurse the pain. Do anything but suppress the pain and pretend that you aren't hurting.

Going No Contact

In Finding Yourself After a Heartbreak there was a whole chapter on going no contact, if you missed it – here's a quick recap.

When you physically cut yourself, the advisable thing to do would be to clean up the wound, cover it well, and ensure that whatever cut you is nowhere near the wound.

Why then, would you want to keep in contact with your ex after a breakup? Why would you want to keep poking at the wound by constantly reminding yourself of the cause of your pain?

Maybe at the height of love, both of you promised to remain friends even if you broke up. It all felt possible at that time because both of you couldn't fathom ever hurting each other. Unfortunately, things change after a breakup.

Even if that breakup or divorce was amicable, and the both of you remained lucid throughout the process, there is no escaping the strong feelings of sadness and anger that come from seeing something you worked so hard on for years' fall apart.

Seeing the relationship you put so much of yourself into crumble in front of your eyes is enough to bring out the strongest reactions from even the most chilled-out among us.

My advice, going no contact with your ex immediately after a breakup is the best way to let the emotional wounds of your heartbreak heal. Delete their number.

Even if you know their number off the top of your head, deleting it will subconsciously display intentionality and a desire to move on.

Block them on social media and resist all urges to create burner accounts to stalk them. In fact, if possible, deactivate your socials and take a social media break for as long as you need to.

But Tristan, what if we are neighbors or work close to each other?

Hmm, that's a challenging one. Indeed, completely avoiding an ex who lives or works close to you might not be entirely feasible. However, you still need to find ways to limit contact as much as possible.

Find different times of going into and coming out of work. If needed, perhaps you can even request to get a different shift just so you do not run the risk of seeing them.

Avoid eating in places where both of you frequented or places where you both could bump into each other. If you are like me, you will likely find that places you used to enjoy as a couple – no longer bring you happiness and you will naturally want to find new venues.

Anything that could make you see or encounter them less, do that.

Reconnect with Previous Hobbies

You dropped your hiking routine, stopped tending to your garden, and began to put less time into your knitting hobby because you wanted to put more time into your relationship. It's easy to feel like a fool once it's all over, but don't.

Losing a part of ourselves when we get into a relationship is nothing to be ashamed of. In fact, it should be expected. However, once it's all over, go back to doing things that you did when single, things that brought you joy.

It is incredible how reconnecting with activities that you did when single can help you process your emotions.

Reconnecting with your old hobby gives you a sense of empowerment, fulfillment, and once again being in control.

If you had no prior hobbies, well you should find one! I have watched people who previously enjoyed nothing more than sitting back and eating junk food turn into fitness enthusiasts after going through a heartbreak. Or formerly homebound folks suddenly become avid travelers.

I suggest finding something that will help you cope with the pain, you're going to need it.

By finding these small pockets of joy you be able to slowly get over your pain and rekindle a passion for life – **and there is nothing sexier than someone who loves life.**

Talk to a Professional

As a human being there is only so much mental and physical pain we can handle, and if and when you feel overwhelmed, find a professional to help you through it.

After we talked, Alfie shared with me that our conversation had helped him see how much just openly talking with someone had contributed to his healing journey. In fact, Alfie went on to say that he started seeing a therapist because he now understood the value of sharing his thoughts in a non-judgemental space.

So, if you feel overwhelmed or unable to regain even a small part of your life because the pain is too much, then seeking professional help could benefit you greatly.

Reflections After a Breakup for Growth Opportunities

At some point during your recovery from divorce, you must pause and ask yourself whether you are learning from your mistakes or simply spiralling.

Intentionally take a long, hard look and think, 'Sure, this hurts, but what can I learn from this?' Once you ask that question, you shift from regret to reflection.

You've seen your marriage crumble after two solid decades, and you don't want those twenty years to feel like time wasted. So, you need to learn some lessons - just like anyone else, including me.

You Were in the Wrong Too

One of the hardest things you may have to do is admit that you also contributed to your marriage ending. Sure, your ex knows fully why they ended the marriage, but through your reflections, you can ask yourself questions about how you may have contributed.

The questions to consider include:

Was I emotionally unavailable?

Did I stop putting effort into myself and the relationship?

Consciously or subconsciously, did I ignore my partner's needs?

Even if you are the one who ended the relationship, it's crucial to ask yourself these questions because they serve as a path to self-awareness and personal growth. Reflecting on your role in the relationship's downfall allows you to gain valuable insights into your behaviour and tendencies.

In recent months, I met an old friend of mine who had just ended a seven-year marriage with the woman he had considered to be the love of his life. Roger said that he just woke up one morning and realized it had been months since he truly enjoyed being with his wife. And so, he decided to end it.

Yet, as we talked, he admitted that a small part of him still regretted ending the marriage.

'I sometimes feel like I pulled the plug too soon. I was impatient and just desperately wanted out," he said.

Rogers story is a lesson for all of us, that even if it was your idea to end the relationship, you still need to self-reflect so that you don't end your next relationship too soon.

It's all in the past, let it go

For a few months after your separation, your just-ended marriage might be all that occupies your thoughts. Thoughts of your ex may seem constant, and memories of what once mattered most fill your mind.

It can take some time to realize that this continuous dwelling on the past is keeping you from moving forward. You find yourself reminiscing about old times instead of seeking lessons from the experience.

It's perfectly normal to reflect on a recently ended relationship; no one would advise against that. However, it's essential to view your past through the lens of learning and personal growth.

There's little to gain from blaming your ex or yourself when looking back. Instead, focus on examining how the relationship evolved and telling yourself, "I wouldn't want to repeat that." Look to the past for lessons, not regrets.

One significant lesson you might discover is the power of forgiveness as a tool for finding closure. It's not about condoning the actions that led to the divorce but rather about releasing the negative energy tied to them.

Forgiving yourself and your ex can free you from resentment and allow you to move forward *without carrying emotional baggage.*

Invest in Yourself

As you work through your emotions and find closure, it's time to focus on creating new goals for yourself. These could be personal, professional, or even related to relationships.

Setting goals gives you a sense of purpose and direction, helping you build a fulfilling post-divorce life.

After my divorce, as I navigated through my own pain and challenges, I realized that there was a significant lack of resources available for individuals facing the same situation. I noticed a gap where real, relatable guidance was needed. I found myself searching for books written by people who had walked a similar path, but I didn't find much.

It was in that moment of realization that I made a firm decision: I would invest in my own growth and well-being, and I would take it upon myself to write a guide that could offer support and insights to others going through a similar journey.

I would have *never* opened this new chapter of my life as an author if I did not take the time to invest in, take care of, and improve who I was.

I clearly remember when I got the idea to write my first book, it was like a light bulb moment, an opportunity to become someone who helped change the lives of people who were in situations like I was.

Of course, not all of us can find ways to invest in ourselves to the point of turning our pain into books. But you can find more things to do for yourself that not only make you navigate the pain but also help you improve your life for the better.

Make time for those who love you

In the previous segment, while I did encourage you to allow yourself some time to feel the pain after a breakup, doing so without a break can lead to anxiety, depression and spiraling into darkness.

Divorce marks a significant transition in your life, reshaping not only your personal world but also the relationships you hold dear. Amidst the emotional turmoil, it's crucial to appreciate that the people who truly care about you - your friends and family - are a source of strength and support during this challenging time.

Remember, divorce can sometimes lead to feelings of isolation, but you're not alone!

Your friends and family are the pillars that can help you regain your sense of belonging and connection. Reach out to them, not only to share your thoughts and feelings but also to just simply enjoy their company. Engaging in social activities will provide a welcome distraction from the stress and emotional weight you might be carrying.

Many divorcees that I've met stated just how much closer they grew to their family and friends after the divorce. A friend of mine John said that sometimes, his friends or siblings would come over to his home and just sit with him and create small talk over coffee.

These actions reminded them just how much love and support he still had in life despite the divorce. And it could also work for you.

When you make time for friends and family, you're not just nurturing relationships—you're **actively participating in your own healing**. The emotional support, laughter, and shared experiences will contribute positively to your overall well-being.

While your journey after your breakup might involve moments of pain and introspection, surrounding yourself with those who love you will bring a sense of comfort and acceptance.

Your interactions might change, but the value of human connection remains constant. By making time for the people who love you, you're investing in the foundation of emotional resilience and growth.

Cherish these moments, for they are the threads that weave your new narrative—a story of healing, transformation, and enduring bonds of love and support.

Open up that journal

In the wake of a divorce, navigating the storm of emotions can be overwhelming. Journaling offers a haven where your thoughts, feelings, and aspirations find a voice. Beyond the ink and paper, journaling becomes a compass guiding you toward healing, growth, and a brighter future.

My friend Oliver experienced a unique, exhilarating sensation when he began to write – a sense of liberation. It was as if he was witnessing his heart's healing process unfolding in real time.

With each word he penned to capture his emotions, it felt like a brick had been lifted from the heavy burden on his shoulders.

The same could work for you too. Begin journaling how you feel each day, nurse the pain in real-time, and watch yourself begin to heal and transform into a new person.

As you pour your emotions onto the page, you'll embark on a journey of self-exploration. Journaling becomes a mirror reflecting your inner world, helping you untangle complex emotions, uncover hidden dreams, and make sense of your new reality.

It's a safe space where your thoughts can flow freely, untethered by judgment, leading you to insights and resolutions.

Journaling also serves as a sanctuary for managing the stress and chaos that often accompany divorce. The act of writing bridges the gap between your thoughts and the tangible world, providing solace and clarity.

Through journaling, you create a mindful haven where you can anchor yourself amidst the tumultuous seas of post-divorce life.

Quick Technique: Stream of Consciousness Journaling for Healing

1. Find a quiet, comfortable space where you won't be interrupted.

2. Set a timer for 10-15 minutes.

3. Open your journal to a blank page.

4. Begin writing without censoring or stopping. Let your thoughts flow freely, even if they seem disjointed.

5. Grammar, punctuation, and coherence **don't** matter. Just keep writing.

6. If you hit a roadblock, write "I don't know what to say" until another thought emerges.

7. Write until the timer chimes.

Remember, this technique isn't about crafting polished prose; it's about channelling your emotions onto the page. Over time, stream of consciousness journaling can be a powerful tool for healing, self-discovery, and embracing your new chapter after divorce.

Processing your emotions and finding closure is an important part of finding love after a breakup, but we are just scratching the surface. In the next chapter, we will look at how to build your confidence before stepping out for dates.

Chapter 2: Building Unshakeable Confidence

Take a moment to imagine that you have decided to go out and begin to meet new people. You wake up one morning full of life. You get ready, put on your best clothes, wear your best smile and spray on your best perfume or aftershave.

As you set out for your rendezvous with your date, you arrive at the meeting spot ahead of schedule. With a bit of extra time on your hands, you take a moment to sit and let your imagination paint a picture of how the date is expected to unfold.

Before you know it, your date arrives, and at that very instant, you find yourself unexpectedly tongue-tied, unable to find the right words to say. A sense of panic washes over you. You begin to wonder, could this sudden loss for words be a lingering effect from your previous heartbreak?

Well, possibly yes.

Healing and moving forward from a previous heartbreak often requires more than just time; it also demands a restoration of your self-confidence[iii].

When you think back to how your past relationship started, it was built upon a foundation of confidence. You had enough belief in yourself to engage and be open with your former partner. Now, as you continue your healing journey, it's crucial to rekindle that inner confidence and rediscover the self-assured person you once were.

Boosting Self-Esteem and Embracing Self-Love

When I spoke to Alfie, he confided in me that the dating jitters were often so bad that he almost never even attempted to talk to people with whom he was romantically interested.

"I just feel like I'm not good enough", he said.

This feeling of not being good enough can cripple your dating experience to such an extent that you may as well stop dating altogether, but that doesn't need to be the case.

It's like putting up a big "Closed for Business" sign on your heart, and I've been there too. But here's the thing – you are ***absolutely deserving of love***, and there are ways to overcome this challenge and make dating once again a positive experience.

How do you embrace yourself and build your confidence?

• Silence Your Inner Critic

That damn voice again! That voice that keeps telling you that you are unworthy, unlovable, and destined to be alone. Yes, that one.

That voice that constantly reminds you of your mistakes, what you did wrong when the previous relationship ended, that voice that tells you that you aren't capable of finding love and happiness again. You need to silence that inner critic that's riding on your back.

Our inner critic often seizes the opportunity to launch an all-out attack, whispering relentless messages about our perceived unworthiness. This internal voice tends to be quite opportunistic.

As mentioned earlier, Oliver embarked on a journey of self-discovery through journaling, and it was in those pages that he learned the art of self-compassion and crafting more realistic self-assessments.

What proved effective for Oliver was a simple yet profound technique: he began documenting those negative thoughts, but instead of framing them in the first person, he expressed them in the second person. For instance, if his inner critic declared, 'You're unworthy and unlovable,' h would record it exactly as it was spoken to him, as if *someone else* were uttering those words, distancing them from his core identity.

To counteract these negative thoughts, hr then composed affirmations in the first person. For example, he would write, 'I may not have been the perfect partner, but I am a complete human being worthy of love and happiness.' This shift in perspective allowed me to detach from the negativity and foster a more compassionate and realistic view of myself.

Research from the University of Arizona[iv] sheds light on the therapeutic power of narrative journaling, particularly in the aftermath of a divorce. It emphasizes how engaging in this practice can offer significant health benefits during the process of healing and recovery.

To achieve this transformation, it will demand your time and unwavering dedication. You must persistently and consistently work on redirecting your thoughts to silence that persistent inner voice. Rest assured, just as it happened for me, your confidence will gradually and steadily make its triumphant return.

• Focus On Your Strengths

'To establish true self-confidence, we must concentrate on our successes and forget about the failures and the negatives in our lives.' - Denis Waitley.

This quote can genuinely resonate with many during the journey of recovery, aiding in the rebuilding of confidence after a breakup.

It's typical to dwell on one's mistakes when a relationship ends, as I've seen in conversations with individuals like Alfie and Roger who faced similar challenges.

However, what's equally important is shifting your focus to acknowledge what you've done right. In those moments when negative emotions overwhelm you, when it feels like you're drowning in a sea of pain, take a moment to identify your strengths - they will provide an anchor for you.

Were you a good listener?

Were you always patient and kind?

Were you always the provider?

In Alfie's reflections, he discovered that throughout his marriage, he embodied patience and empathy, qualities he genuinely values in himself. Loyalty was at the core of his commitment, and he took immense pride in being the primary provider for both his partner and himself. These are aspects of his character that he holds in high esteem and takes pride in!

For those who find themselves in a similar situation, I encourage you to concentrate on the positive aspects of your role as a partner. Recognizing your strengths in this context can be empowering. I strongly recommend that you not only continue to nurture these strengths but also actively work on rectifying any shortcomings you may have identified. It's a constructive path toward personal growth and improved relationships.

- **Improve Your Posture**

Wait what? you might ask, but let's dig a little deeper.

Many people during times of heartbreak often unconsciously exhibit body language that mirrors their inner emotional turmoil. This phenomenon isn't typically deliberate; it tends to occur naturally.

These individuals frequently display slouched shoulders, a sunken chest, and feet that seem to drag along the ground, as if they're bearing a considerable weight – which, in a way, they are.

However, purposefully changing or enhancing your body language can have a positive effect on your state of mind and self-perception.

[Research done by Ohio State University](#) [v] in 2009 found that a good posture wasn't just good for your physical body but it also gave you more **confidence in your thoughts**.

In the study, researchers discovered that individuals who maintained an upright posture were more inclined to have confidence in the opinions they penned down. Conversely, those who slouched at their desks exhibited less conviction about what they wrote.

What this research teaches us it that if you're aiming to boost your self-confidence, focusing on enhancing your body language and posture is key. It's essential to release the burden of heartbreak, or at the very least, prevent it from dragging you down.

So, drop the slouch! Begin to stand up straight, sit upright, and hold your head high. Even when you do not feel confident enough, as the saying goes, fake it till you make it.

Train your body to hold confident postures, and your mind will soon follow.

- **View Yourself as Equal to Others**

After going through a breakup and observing all the happy couples while you're out and about, it can heighten emotions of inadequacy, failure and self-doubt. Such moments may lead you to question whether you'll ever have the chance to experience a loving relationship ever again.

With this mindset, going on dates becomes an intimidating prospect. Dating necessitates confidence, and in this state of mind, it can feel like a daunting hurdle because the fear of failure looms large, potentially sabotaging any initial attempts.

"Love yourself first and everything else falls into line. You really have to love yourself to get anything done in this world." - Lucille Ball

Think about this metaphor: If you were holding a $100 bill and it got crumpled up, stepped on, even torn slightly – would it lose its value? Absolutely not! The same applies to you; life may crumple you, step on you or even tear at your heartstrings but remember, like the $100 bill, your value remains intact.

Much like a resilient $100 bill that retains its worth, you too can overcome life's crumples and challenges while preserving your inherent value. When life crumples, steps on, or tugs at your heartstrings, remember that your intrinsic worth remains unaltered.

To smooth out those metaphorical wrinkles, consider the simple yet powerful act of jotting down the qualities that make you a captivating and engaging individual. These unique traits are the keys to restoring your self-confidence and embracing your authentic self, no matter what life throws your way.

- **Visualize How You Want to Feel**

In the journey of healing and personal growth, another powerful tool you can harness is the art of visualization[vi]. It's like creating a mental movie that transports you to a space of your own choosing, allowing you to experience emotions and situations in a positive and impactful way.

When you start visualizing how you want your future to be, you begin to see yourself as a confident, self-assured, and outgoing person.

It's more than just a daydream; you'll feel the confidence of this envisioned persona radiate through you when you decide to go out on a date. It's as if, by thinking of yourself more positively, you're actively shaping your own reality and opening the door to newfound self-assurance.

Picture this, you are out on a date with a wonderful person, they are attentive and beautiful. You know exactly the right things to say, you look good and you feel confident. Your date is getting more and more comfortable with you and things are going well.

Seems idealistic, doesn't it? Well, it's something that you can actually do.

Take 5-10 minutes each day, close your eyes, and imagine how you would wish for your ideal date to go. Even when you do not have someone in mind, imagine how you would present yourself to someone you like.

What will your posture be like? What would you say, and how would you say it?

How would you wish your body to feel at that moment?

What would you want to be thinking at any given time?

Let's give it a try.

Find a comfortable and quiet space to sit or lie down. Close your eyes and take a deep breath, letting go of any tension. Imagine that you're about to experience a positive and uplifting date that leaves you feeling refreshed and joyful. Let your imagination guide you through this visualization journey:

Step 1: Setting the Scene

Visualize the location of your positive date. It might be a cosy café, a scenic park, or a charming art gallery. Envision yourself arriving at this place, feeling excited and open to the experience.

Step 2: Embracing the Moment

As you step into the venue, take a moment to absorb the atmosphere around you. Notice the sights, sounds, and smells that surround you. Allow yourself to fully embrace the present moment.

Step 3: Engaging Conversation

Imagine engaging in a conversation with your date. Visualize yourself sharing stories, laughing, and connecting on a genuine level. Feel the positive energy of the conversation lifting your spirits.

Step 4: Authentic Connection

Visualize the connection deepening as you and your date share personal experiences and thoughts. Feel a sense of understanding and warmth between you. Allow yourself to be fully present and engaged.

Step 5: Inner Confidence

Picture yourself feeling confident and comfortable in your own skin. Imagine your inner dialogue being kind and supportive, boosting your self-assurance. Let go of any self-doubt and embrace a sense of inner strength.

Step 6: Enjoying Activities

Engage in activities that bring joy to the date. Whether it's enjoying delicious food, exploring art, or taking a leisurely stroll, savour each moment. Feel a sense of enjoyment and gratitude for the experience.

Step 7: Positive Emotions

Visualize a wave of positive emotions washing over you. Feel happiness, contentment, and a genuine sense of connection with your date. Imagine these emotions as a warm and radiant light within your heart.

Step 8: Gratitude and Reflection

As the date comes to an end, take a moment to reflect on the positive moments you've shared. Visualize yourself expressing gratitude for the experience and feeling thankful for the connection you've made.

Step 9: Carrying the Positivity

Imagine leaving the venue with a heart full of positivity. Feel the uplifting energy of the date accompanying you as you continue your day. Carry this positivity with you, radiating it to those you interact with.

Step 10: Open Your Eyes

Slowly open your eyes and take a deep breath. Allow the feelings of joy, connection, and confidence from the visualization to linger. Carry this positive energy with you as you move forward, knowing that you have the power to create uplifting experiences in your life.

• Focus More On How You Feel

Here's a straightforward truth: You don't hold the reins over someone else's feelings towards you. It might be a bit disappointing to hear, but that's simply the way it goes.

In the world of dating, many folks never quite grasp this concept, but it's essential to understand that you can't manipulate someone's feelings to like you more. I'm here to share with you the reality that controlling how others feel about you is *beyond your influence.*

What you can do, however, is ***focus on your own feelings and decide if you genuinely like the other person***.

If you enter the dating scene with the sole purpose of trying to make the other person like you, you may find yourself resorting to inauthenticity, dishonesty, and, perhaps even worse, manipulation, which leads you away from being your true self.

Let me clarify something: it's natural to want the person you're dating to like you. However, when your primary focus becomes making them like you at any cost, it can lead to manipulation because you're not being your genuine self.

Instead, focus more on how you feel about them. This way, you feel empowered and participate in the progression of that relationship rather than leaving the whole process in the hands of the other person.

You will bring your authentic self to the table because you will feel more confident in your feelings, and, if the other person is as confident in their feelings as you are, it helps progress the relationship smoothly and honestly.

Speaking of authenticity, staying true to yourself is yet another essential part of building your self-confidence. So, how do you work towards being authentic and overcoming your shame and insecurities?

Stepping into Your Authentic Self

Authenticity is the biggest sign of confidence in a person. That ability to remain true to yourself despite everything going on around you is remarkable.

But what is Authenticity?

I've had the chance to engage with many individuals who are re-entering the dating world. Interestingly, a substantial portion of them encounter difficulties in forging deep connections.

"I have tried to peak their interest, tried all the tips and tricks in the dating books, but somehow I can't get people to like me," this person would say.

*"Have you tried – **just being yourself**?"* I ask.

There is often a look of shock after I say this, as though I have said something very profound.

You see, much of the messaging we get from dating will often seem to suggest that we need to change ourselves in order to be liked. But here is the thing – when looking to date and find someone for you, being authentic is the best strategy[vii] to use if you are to succeed in finding your match.

What if, after all the effort, you end up in a new relationship where you can't truly be yourself? Imagine this scenario: you manage to attract someone's interest by portraying an exaggerated version of yourself that isn't authentic.

You might get swept up in the excitement of the initial attraction, but sooner or later, the facade will start to crumble. The real you will emerge, and if your true self doesn't align with the image you've projected, the foundation of the relationship becomes shaky.

However, if you are true to yourself, then you are being authentic.

Authenticity refers to **having a keen awareness of yourself**, what you stand for and expressing yourself openly and honestly. It means being true to yourself and acting consistently with your inner values and character.

In dating, being authentic could be the difference between finding your match or ending up with someone just because they are available.

I imagine that when looking for a date, you are looking for someone whose values align with yours, someone with whom you share a lot in common. And that will often be easier to do when you are authentic.

But how do you build this authenticity, especially after a heartbreak?

- **Explore Your Values**

Embarking on the journey of dating after a divorce is a transformative experience that allows you to rediscover yourself and your values. It's a time to reflect on the lessons learned, both from the past relationship and the person you've become. As you step into this new chapter, exploring your values becomes paramount.

What do you stand for?

What are your non-negotiables?

What are the intrinsic things that matter most to you?

The revelations that come to us during times of heartbreak will often be very illuminating and eye-opening. On a personal level, I discovered just how determined I was after my divorce, and it was that determination that helped me rebuild my life afterward.

You, like many, can discover your own core values when faced with such challenges. Take a moment to sit down and explore your life by asking a few critical questions:

When did you feel alive the most, and what made you feel that way??

What qualities about yourself do you hold dear?

What values do you believe in?

What qualities do you admire in other people?

What do you like about a romantic partner?

How would you like to pursue your ideal relationship?

As you engage in this introspective journey and respond candidly, you'll unearth your own set of values, paving the way for a more authentic version of yourself to shine through. Visit www.tristanbrody.com[viii] if you would like a free values worksheet.

• Become More in Touch with Your Emotions

Well, thank you Tristan, as if the pain of heartbreak isn't enough, I need to feel every other emotion, I hear you say, but let me explain.

Our ability to experience a wide range of emotions is both a blessing and a curse. During tough moments like heartbreak, these emotions will often be very hard to pin down and express. It's why heartbreak hurts so much.

When we don't know how to best express these emotions, they can have a negative impact on our mental health. Becoming more in touch with your emotions doesn't mean feeling more pain from heartbreak. Instead, it involves mastering these emotions so that they don't have total control over you.

You know that person who damages their ex's car, house or goes out of their way to stick it up to their ex? Well, you don't want to be that person. And, to stop that from becoming you, you need to be more in touch with your emotions.

Enter **Mindfulness.**

Many people never truly realize just how much the world is passing them by until they begin practicing mindfulness. It's as though a whole new world opens up in front of their eyes.

Mindfulness also brings awareness to one's emotions, helping recognize the onset of feelings without self-judgment. Through mindfulness, they allow themselves to detach from their emotions.

This way, they can deal with their emotions rather than having them control their actions. Here's a simple mindfulness practice you can try:

Focused Breathing Meditation:

1. Find a quiet and comfortable place to sit or lie down.

2. Close your eyes if you feel comfortable doing so, or maintain a soft gaze in front of you.

3. Begin by taking a few deep breaths to relax your body.

4. Shift your attention to your breath. Pay close attention to the sensation of your breath entering and leaving your nostrils or the rise and fall of your chest or abdomen.

5. As you breathe in and out, thoughts may naturally arise. Acknowledge these thoughts without judgment, and then gently guide your focus back to your breath.

6. Continue to concentrate on your breath for a predetermined amount of time, such as 5 or 10 minutes, or longer if you prefer.

7. If your mind starts to wander, which is entirely normal, gently redirect your attention to your breath each time.

8. Gradually, as you practice, you may notice a greater sense of calm and relaxation.

This basic mindfulness exercise can help you develop the skill of staying present and focused, ultimately enhancing your ability to manage stress and become more attuned to the world around you.

Visit https://www.youtube.com/@tristanbrody for free guided mediations and mindfulness videos.

- **Set Clear Boundaries**

Imagine a pivotal moment in your journey towards authenticity: a time when you recognized the importance of setting boundaries. Let's consider an example to illustrate this.

After her relationship ended, Sarah found herself grappling with the idea of redefining her boundaries. While she had always been adept at asserting her limits, the aftermath of her breakup left her questioning how to navigate this terrain again.

Sarah's experience sheds light on a universal challenge that many face. Often, after parting ways with a partner, the inclination to compromise boundaries arises as a way to avoid conflict or further discomfort.

However, this compromise can inadvertently disconnect you from your authentic self. It's as though you're relinquishing a part of your identity in an attempt to preserve the peace.

Now, picture this scenario: instead of relinquishing her boundaries, Sarah began to re-establish them with newfound clarity. She recognized the significance of being assertive about her needs, values, and personal limits.

This self-awareness prompted her to learn effective communication techniques, ensuring her boundaries were understood by potential partners.

You may also find yourself in a similar predicament, unsure of how to recalibrate your boundaries in the dating world. The truth is, healthy boundaries signify self-care and respect.

They're not about building walls or keeping potential partners at bay but rather about defining where you draw the line in fostering authentic relationships.

And no, setting healthy boundaries doesn't mean having a wall that doesn't let people into your life. Rather, it is knowing where you draw the limit to have authentic relationships.

Boundaries allow you to nurture connections with potential partners who genuinely respect, appreciate, and accept you for yourself. They help you uphold your sense of self so you don't lose your true self or feel like conforming to people's expectations to date them.

If a person is right for you, they will respect the version of yourself you bring to relationships and won't feel the need to change you. Setting and implementing boundaries are vital to building unwavering confidence and finding love with someone who values your authentic self.

- **Let Go Perfectionism**

As you sit there in pain, you tell yourself that you will not let the next relationship end up like the previous one. You will be perfect, and everything will be alright.

The question is, who are you kidding?

Through this belief in perfection, you will watch your every action, your every thought. You will seek to control everything and everyone, which is almost the complete opposite of living authentically.

Perfectionism can be a silent saboteur, hindering progress and stifling creativity.

Let's take Jordan as a case in point. Jordan found themselves caught in the same challenging cycle. The quest for flawlessness led them to meticulously plan their attire and to mirror the looks of people showcased in glossy magazines.

All this effort was in pursuit of embodying what they believed was the image of a divorcee stepping back into the dating arena.

Yet, beneath the polished exterior, Jordan couldn't escape the feeling of being a stranger to themselves. It was akin to donning a mask, a mask that concealed their genuine essence and imperfections.

Soon, Jordan came to realize that as imperfect as they were, they needed to embrace it. They needed to bring their *authentic* best self to dates, not their *perfect* self. As soon as Jordan made peace with that, it felt as though a burden had been taken off their shoulders.

You have to realize and accept one thing; **imperfections make you unique.** Celebrate your uniqueness and learn to love strengths, quirks, and all. Recognize that setbacks and mistakes are natural and provide valuable learning and growth opportunities.

When you release perfectionism, you will feel liberated. You will freely express your need, want, and limits without fearing judgment.

Letting go of perfectionism allows you to be true to your desires and feelings, even if they do not conform to other people's expectations. Embracing imperfection will enable you to entice people who appreciate your authentic self, creating more fulfilling and genuine relationships.

Release perfectionism and open doors for the endless opportunities and possibilities that await you.

- **Release Comparison**

During this challenging period, you might be tempted to compare yourself and your failed relationship with those of others.

You might say, "So and so is still happy with their partner. Why can't I be like them?" It happens, but it is a trap to erode your self-confidence and damage your authenticity. This is because we all have unique and different journeys, and there is no set manual or guide to love, or life.

You will want to question your self-worth and reflect on your failed relationship by using other people's relationships for comparison, but this only prevents you from embracing your true self. Instead, pay more attention to your development and growth.

How? You may wonder.

Ensure you celebrate all your milestones and accomplishments in all aspects of your life, regardless of how small or big. Also, recognize your best qualities and strengths and use them to your advantage.

For example, if you are kind-hearted, instead of comparing yourself with another less-kind person and how they still are in a happy relationship, nurture your kind heart with acts of kindness and celebrate whenever you use that trait to connect with others and bring smiles to their faces.

When you stop seeking validation and embrace your true personality instead, you will start promoting your authentic self. You will liberate yourself from setting unrealistic goals and expectations for yourself and others.

Remember that everyone has their unique path, and what works for others might not work for you. We all are trying to find our paths to growth and self-discovery; the breakup is just a challenge in your life journey and is there to help you learn and become better and stronger.

So, embrace every step of the way and the person you are becoming. When you do this, you will stop comparing yourself with others, develop the courage to connect with your authentic self, and attract people who honor and appreciate you for who you are.

- **Be Self-Compassionate**

The post-breakup journey is emotionally challenging and can leave you criticizing and blaming yourself.

Many of the people I've encountered who have experienced divorce or the end of a long-term relationship tend to be quite tough on themselves. I empathize with their perspective, and if you're also grappling with showing self-compassion, I get you.

Being self-compassionate is essential to building authenticity and confidence. If a friend were in the same situation as you, you would be kind, understanding and supportive as you helped them get through the breakup challenges. Offer the same kindness and support to yourself!

Being compassionate with yourself lets you foster a loving and positive connection with yourself. It helps you realize that you deserve happiness and love from yourself, those in your life, and those to come.

Remember: Self-compassion is not avoiding growth or self-indulgence. Rather, it's about being your own number one support system and understanding during this challenging period, and recognizing that you deserve acceptance and love, just as you are.

- **Improve How You Communicate**

The end of one relationship doesn't mark the end of love in your life. In fact, it can often be a gateway to finding a more profound, fulfilling bond. But how can you ensure that this time around things will work out better? It all starts with communication.

Interestingly, research[ix] has found that 9 out of 10 conversations missed the mark, resulting in conflicts, confusion, and general misunderstanding. That's a pretty huge percentage!

How good of a communicator were you in your last relationship?

Roger realized that he may not have been a keen listener because he would sometimes be flicking through the TV or scrolling on his phone when his partner spoke to him. That is not a flattering indictment when he looks back, but he knows moving forward he won't do that in his next relationship.

Sit back and think back to how you communicate. Ask yourself:

- ✓ Do you express how you feel?
- ✓ If so, how do you express it?
- ✓ How do you communicate your feelings if you don't express them?

A common misconception regarding effective communication is believing that you must always avoid conflict at all costs, this couldn't be further from truth! Disagreements are a normal part healthy relationship, its handling them constructively that fosters growth and mutual respect among partners.

Let's take Jane and Tom as an example; both are divorcees who've found solace in each other's company after their marriages ended bitterly due to poor communication. They're determined not to repeat their past mistakes but are unsure where to start.

After some soul-searching and research, they realize that effective communication is like learning a new language; it requires practice, patience, and understanding.

In the course of her research, Jane encounters a captivating concept known as 'communication style[x].' She discovers that these styles predominantly fall into four categories: passive, aggressive, passive-aggressive, and assertive. Recognizing which style resonates with each of them becomes the initial stride toward enhancing their interactions.

Tom on the other hand was scrolling through his news feed, when he stumbled upon an article about 'active listening'. He learned how important it is for communication in relationships by making him feel heard and understood by his partner.

If you are passive-aggressive, understand that you won't get much luck in dating by holding back your feelings. In fact, you may send the other person running a mile. You'll need to learn how to express joy, displeasure, or frustration with the other person in a healthy way.

One tip to avoid coming off as blaming the other person, learn to use I instead of you. For example, instead of saying, "You never listen to me," you could say, "I feel unheard when I share my thoughts." This way, you're expressing your feelings without directly attributing blame to the other person.

Embracing authenticity and cultivating self-love lays the foundation for a more rewarding journey back into the world of dating. When you're truly comfortable in your own skin and have a deep appreciation for your own worth, you radiate confidence and attract genuine connections.

This self-assured approach empowers you to engage in dating with a clear sense of what you're seeking and what you have to offer, creating a healthier and more fulfilling experience for both yourself and potential partners.

Chapter 3: Navigating the World of Online Dating

Many readers, just like you, are people that got married during a time when online dating was a mystery.

Sure, some early adopters had embraced it, but for the most of us, it was something that we never took interest in. Instead, many of these people, me included, met our partners the traditional way.

Today, the vast number of options that you have already make online dating intimidating for many, especially for divorcees coming off a very long marriage that began during the 1990's or even earlier; at a time when saying you met someone online was enough to have people question your sanity.

But jokes aside, online dating has completely changed the dating landscape and is also very different from what it was. If that is the route that you want to take, then understanding how to go about it is vital.

Finding The Best App for You

When Alfie first tried online dating, it felt like a surreal new world. So new was it to him that after creating his profile, he completely forgot about it, and it was only a few weeks later that he remembered he had it.

Alfie opened the app to a number of messages, which all represented missed opportunities to meet someone new. But you don't need to fail on your first try like him.

Despite their failure, dating apps are now a mainstay in the dating world, but with so many different options available, choosing the best one for you can be challenging. Below, we look at how to find the best app for you.

- **What Are You Looking for?**

At the start of online dating, many people will often not be looking for something serious; at least that is what I observed from people I've met.

For many, it is a process of sifting through various apps, going through trial and error until they learned which apps served their needs at a given time. And this is also what you need to understand.

The first question you need to ask yourself when choosing a dating app is what it is you are looking for. While most dating apps promise to match you with your perfect mate, some will often do this task better than others.

For example, **eHarmony** has gained a reputation as an app best suited for meeting long-term, potential-marriage partners. It connects people with similarly matched people for long-term relationships; so, if you want a long-term relationship, eHarmony could be your first choice.

Match.com is also great for meeting long-term partners, especially if you are older. It is an app in which the more questions you answer, the better your match becomes.

If you are a woman and would wish to meet someone on your terms, then **Bumble** is the app for you. The app encourages women to make the first move on a person they find attractive, which can be significant in helping you date on your terms instead of waiting on the sidelines to be approached. It also prevents men making the first move and potentially bombarding you.

If you are looking to date casually, perhaps because you feel you do not have it in you to get into anything serious, then **Tinder** is great for you.

Knowing your intentions[xi] will make navigating the world of online dating a lot easier because you will be on apps that align with what you want, rather than simply downloading several apps and then getting crippled by havoc of choice.

- **Consider The Matching Formula**

When selecting a dating app, consider the filters they use to narrow the search and whether they suit your liking. Different dating apps will use other metrics for compatibility; thus, you should find one whose metrics are much closer to what you want.

For example:

- Do you wish to be limited to potential partners in your location simply?

- Do you want to be matched based on hobbies and other interests or entirely based on the kind of relationship you want to pursue?

Apps like **OkCupid** will often provide you with recommended matches once you have set your profile, meaning that whatever you put on your profile is one of the significant criteria they will use to filter recommended matches.

You may need to experiment to see which platform has the most features that appeal to you before signing up for any of them.

- **Consider Subscription Options**

Many dating apps will often say that they are free, and they usually are, but you also need to consider whether you are getting the value you want out of that app in its free features or whether you need to subscribe to its premium offer.

I learnt this the hard way when I signed up for some 'free' apps only to find that they had hidden the features that I needed the most behind the subscription.

If you decide to use a free version of an app, ensure that the one you choose does not hide most of the features that you would consider necessary to you in its paid plans.

For example, if you would wish to be matched on long-term compatibility, but the app only has this in its subscription package, then you don't need that app unless you are willing to pay.

Compare different apps and platforms and consider which features are best for free or at an affordable subscription rate you would be willing to pay for.

- **Decide On Your Deal-Breaker On the App**

When choosing an app, also consider what you wouldn't tolerate from the app, even when it seems to be the best for you. I quickly let go of apps that did not serve my needs.

For example, does the app have a reputation for data gathering? Does the app have too many advertisements and keeps pushing you to its subscription plan? Is the app solely focused on appearances?

Recently, some apps[xii] have gained a reputation for focusing more on pushing attractive people and less on other qualities.

- **Always Consider Reviews**

While reviews don't tell the whole story, they are essential to understanding whether the app you want to use does what it's supposed to or is below expectations.

I know that you will easily get carried away by reviews that focus on technical issues. 'This app is slow, it consumes too much data' and so on. And while that's fine, focus a lot more of your attention on how useful the app is to those using it.

For example, the app hides too many great features being hidden behind subscriptions or bad experiences from users, such as the app being a hub for creeps and criminals.

While these apps will probably not do many background checks, if an app gains a reputation for being used a lot by people with sinister intentions, then that is not an app you want to use to try and rekindle your dating life.

However, remember not to have too many such apps on your phone. I wrongly believed that having more apps meant more options and many people I have met trying to date again also wrongly believe this.

However, when we shared our experience, we quickly realized that we were harming our ability to date by having too many apps. This is because it meant that we had a hard time choosing dates and this made dating a lot more stressful and less fun.

You can have two apps at most, but even one is still more than sufficient, primarily if it fulfils most of your preferences and intentions. And while you're at it, remember that your profile is your most significant selling point in the online dating world.

Crafting an Appealing and Genuine Online Dating Profile

After first signing up on an online dating app, I spent the first few hours regularly changing up my profile. I had no idea what I needed to do so I often would just change things that came to mind.

Crafting an online dating profile is one of the most challenging parts of online dating. I would state that it is a lot more complex than even selecting the best dating app.

If you've spent enough time on the internet, you have often seen the jokes around people being left dumbfounded when asked to describe themselves in a job interview. The is also the case when creating a genuine profile.

If you are not careful, you could create a dating profile that could make potential dates skip because they think you are incompatible with them or, worse still, boring. And you do not want that.

So, here is what I found out about creating a profile that will get you messages too:

- **Username**

The first and critical stage of online dating is selecting a username. Of course, for security reasons, you should never use your full name, but that does not mean that you should not be creative with your username.

Many people, especially those younger or maybe new to the whole scene, would probably go for names that make them seem fun and quirky but often come off as desperate and corny.

This is many people's first mistake. A corny name sounds funny in your head but I assure you, nothing makes a potential date swipe past your profile quicker than an embarrassing username.

Avoid names that sound sexually suggestive or seem to imply sexual activity. ***Hotguy69*** or ***BigDickJohn*** states that it is suitable for a profile on a hook-up site but not on a serious dating profile.

Believe me when I say that such usernames will turn away 9 out of 10 potential matches, and the one who won't be turned away will probably be curious as to why you think such a name would fly on a serious dating app.

Instead, choose a username that hints at the kind of person you are. The name could indicate a hobby, such as Soccerguy or Flowergirl, GardenQueen, or a wordplay or pun on your name. For example, a username such as IronSmith or Smithoperator could work if your surname is Smith.

They sound corny, true, but they are playful and hint at your playful personality. You could also use pop culture references, hinting at what you enjoy. For example, a handle that hints at this interest could work if you want Star Wars. So, if your name is James, you could call yourself JamesBobbatFett and such.

Also, **avoid adding numbers at the end of your handle** because it can come off as boring, and most people associate handles with numbers at the end with bots. Someone swiping left on your profile because they don't like you is bad enough, but them thinking you are a bot is unacceptable.

- **Writing A Winning Bio**

Writing a bio is also another crucial step to getting the best out of online dating.

Many divorcees battle whether or not they should include the fact that they are divorced on their bio. I would suggest that you consider what you are looking for.

If you are looking to date for fun, then there is no need to include it. However, if your date asks, then you can reveal it.

You see, once you nail the username, your biography is what sells you. Now, as if finding a great username is not hard enough, writing down your bio is one of the most challenging parts of online dating.

At this point, when you are recovering from a heartbreak, you will get stuck because it would remind you of the person you were before your heartbreak.

Writing a winning bio has a few critical formulas.

Honesty and Authenticity

The first step towards creating a winning bio is simply being honest and authentic. I know there is pressure to try to make your life a lot more interesting and exciting than it is, but you should be aware that most people live ordinary lives, just like you.

So, there is no need to try and embellish your life with lies. You could exaggerate your bio a little but not enough for it to become a lie.

You might say that by not including that I am divorced at first was not authentic, but I was very much willing to let my date know about it when we met and they were curious about my situation.

Also, be honest about your intentions. It is a win for everyone involved if you are forthright about your preferences in your bio. If you are looking for a casual fling, then mention that upfront.

If you want a long-term commitment, also say that. This information gives potential matches a better idea of whether or not you are compatible. So, for me, while I did not include my divorce information at first, I did mention that I wasn't looking for something serious.

However, even as you are honest and authentic, keep away some things from the bio. For example, when looking for a long-term commitment, do not mention how many children you would want to have in the future or how much money a potential partner should make.

Most people shy away from these topics when it comes to online dating. I also imagine you wouldn't bring these topics up when meeting someone for a real-life first date, so why put it on your profile?

That is a topic reserved for when the both of you see a future in your relationship, which varies from person to person, but it often is rarely the first or even second date.

Tell a Story

When my friend Cary tried online dating, she turned her online dating bio into a story, linking parts of her life together like a narrative. This was in a bid to appear more relatable.

And guess what? It worked!

Most of the messages Cary would read were from people who thought that her life sounded very interesting and they wanted to meet them, and this could work for you too.

Instead of listing your interests or hobbies, write them as a story. For example, you're an accountant who loves gardening, traveling, and reading.

Rather than simply listing down these hobbies, which would make for a predictable and boring read, write it in the form of a story as below:

'So, you want to know my interests, huh? Well, I am an accountant working six out of seven days. Due to the stress of such a job, I enjoy doing things that help me relax and take my mind off work, which is why gardening is for me.

I especially love the poppy and cross berry, two pretty flower plants representing the simple joys I find in gardening.

When I want to unplug, I love to travel. I especially love coastal towns and exploring sandy beaches and the vast ocean. In the evenings, I enjoy curling up with a fiction book (horror and thrillers are my favorite genres) and reading them by the fireplace.'

The above is an example of making your principal write-up in the bio much more exciting and engaging. Of course, you'll need to keep an eye on the word count to have all your most important interests and hobbies before the word count is up.

From time to time, edit your profile and bio. Shorten your story if you need to, and edit out any grammatical or spelling mistakes or typos.

While it might seem pedantic, many people often skip a profile that seems poorly put together because they perceive it as a lack of effort or care on your part. It might also come off as not being confident enough.

Things to Avoid

As you write your profile, remember that you should avoid making these mistakes that many people make:

1. Don't dwell on the negatives. Listing down your deal breakers might seem like a good idea, but you come off as a tiring person to be around. List things you love and enjoy, not those you don't.

2. Be confident, not arrogant. Unfortunately, most people do not know how to be satisfied without appearing arrogant. When you write down something significant about yourself, re-read it from a detached perspective to see how it sounds. Don't overly praise your abilities or physical appearance; you can mention them and take pride in them without being arrogant.

3. *Work your way around clichés*. It's nearly impossible to completely steer clear of them, but when possible, try to do so. For instance, if you're passionate about hiking, it's almost inevitable to mention it since it's a common interest. Similarly, if 'dining out' with friends is your thing, you don't have to leave it out. However, the key is to find a unique approach. Share your favorite hiking trail and what sets it apart in your eyes. Always inject a touch of personalization into the cliché to make it shine.

4. *Don't leave blanks*. Many people often want to come off as mysterious to intrigue potential matches, but leaving blanks in any section of your profile will often be interpreted as lazy. So, even if you have to get a bit creative with information and approach, do that. It will show that you are willing to put in the effort.

- **Selecting Pictures**

Selecting the best pictures for your profile is another challenging part of online dating. Your photo[xiii] is why many people will either make the next move or keep scrolling. Your profile needs to be a picture that invites potential matches to you.

Below is how to choose the best photos for your profile.

Close-Up Selfie

For your profile, select a close-up selfie in a well-lit area with your eyes visible and staring directly at the camera. You want your eyes visible in your profile picture because it establishes trust and makes you friendlier with potential matches.

It needs to be a selfie or other informal close-up photo rather than a passport so that you don't come off as too formal. This is a dating site, not LinkedIn - so your profile picture needs to be a bit more playful.

Ensure that the selected images are high resolution and clear. Avoid blurry or low-res images, which don't correctly reveal who you are.

Use Action Shots

You can also go down the route of action shots, which, according to Bumble, revealed that users got more likes on the app. Pictures of you doing your favorite hobby work like a charm, whether it's playing sports, playing the guitar, or out on the hiking trail.

My first profile picture was of me out hiking, and this was mentioned by many of my potential dates as one of the reasons they got in touch. It was my authentic self, reaching out through the picture!

Be The Only Person in The Main Photo

Even as you aim for action shots, ensure that you are the only person in the main photo and most of the pictures. This is to ensure that potential matches know who you are.

However, you can include one or two social shots with family or friends. For privacy, block out their faces in the shared image.

Remember that your profile is the primary connection between you and your potential matches. Thus, it would help if you put as much effort into it as you would in your appearances when going out for an actual date. If not, you will not get suitable matches in the various online dating apps.

Most of all Stay Safe!

Online dating has become an increasingly popular way to meet potential partners, but it's crucial to prioritize safety, especially when sharing personal information. One fundamental principle for online daters is to practice "string safe" behaviour. String safe essentially means being cautious and vigilant in your online interactions to protect yourself from potential risks.

First and foremost, when using online dating platforms, never share personal information like your home address, phone number, or financial details with someone you've just met online. This information can be exploited for malicious purposes, and it's best to keep it confidential until you've established a strong level of trust. Instead, communicate within the platform's messaging system, which provides a layer of anonymity and security.

Secondly, practice "string safe" by being selective about the information you reveal in your dating profile. While it's important to provide enough details to give potential matches a sense of who you are, avoid oversharing. Revealing too much personal information upfront can make you vulnerable to scammers or individuals with ill intentions.

Strike a balance between showcasing your personality and maintaining your privacy.

Lastly, when you decide to meet someone in person from an online dating platform, prioritize your safety by choosing a public location for the first date. Inform a trusted friend or family member about your plans and share your date's contact information with them. It's always wise to have a safety net in place, just in case. By practicing "string safe" online dating, you can navigate the world of online romance with confidence and protect yourself from potential risks.

Chapter 4: Effective Communication and Boundaries

There was this one time, during one of my many trips for work purposes, when I met someone whom we will call Nelly.

Nelly was in a long-term committed relationship which according to her, was going quite well. However, Nelly confided in me that while the relationship was great, since the beginning of their relationship, she had had a hard time communicating pressing matters with her partner.

Their relationship had started on the right footing, but the more the two stayed together, the less they were able to speak clearly about what their needs were.

They never spoke about boundaries and it was not uncommon for them to find themselves in each other's spaces, something that, while Nelly wasn't opposed to, said that she would have loved more if they had spoken about it.

Nelly is not alone in this. Most of us are often very fearful of speaking our minds to someone we love for fear of wronging them. Yet, to build a proper, functioning relationship, communication is of the essence.

How to Build Effective Communication Skills in Dating

What does the word communication evoke in you? I want to believe that you see it as speaking clearly what you mean. But that is merely a part of communication.

Communicating encompasses every part of building a rapport with the other person and thus, involves you building all essential skills of communication. It affects our overall satisfaction[xiv] in the relationship. What skills are these?

- **Active Listening**

We touched lightly on this earlier, but I want to dive deeper into this chapter.

Remember Alfie who realized that he was not a very good listener in his marriage after my divorce? This realization ate him to pieces because he often never interrupted his previous partner when she spoke.

Many of you may also come to this realization; knowing that while you often are silent when your partner speaks, you actually aren't listening to them at all.

You see, active listening is more than just letting the other person speak. It is an art and skill built over time where you genuinely pay attention to what the other person is saying.

It is more than just waiting for your turn to speak, which is what I and I believe most of us, engage in.

So how do you become an active listener when on dates?

- Clear your mind of anticipatory thoughts and focus more on what the other person is saying.

- Pay attention to their words, tone of voice, and how they present the information.

- Listen to them without judgment and as though you have nothing else important to do.

Additionally:

Always keep the other person's face in sight. To avoid a wandering mind, whenever your date is talking to you, ensure that you are looking at them. Make frequent and prolonged eye contact; even when you look away, ensure their face is still within your eyesight. Looking at the person speaking to you makes you pay more attention to what they are saying.

Clear your mind. Try not to focus on your thoughts or what you will say next. Instead, sit in silence and put your mind firmly into what the other person is saying. Whenever your mind wanders, bring it back to the conversation.

Do not judge. Reserve your judgment as you listen to the other person. If they say something you disagree with, note it down mentally and continue listening. Do not interrupt and do not dwell on it or you will lose track of the conversation.

Active listening is a skill that takes time to develop, and no doubt you will find yourself stumbling along the way. However, remain persistent, and you will find that you will become a better listener with each date you go to.

- **Speak with Clarity**

Now we come to what many of us picture when we hear communication.

Many of us are often never direct in saying what we think, what we need or want. Have you ever found yourself in a situation where the other person is losing their patience when you speak?

If you are constantly being told 'get to the point', then you are someone struggling to speak with clarity.

Often, this could be down to lacking proper communication skills but it could also be a sign of lacking confidence in telling the other person exactly what you feel. When on a date, this can lead to a lot of misunderstandings.

So, you should also learn how to speak clearly and concisely if you are to have any success in the dating world

For example, if you are not feeling the other person as much, but they are hoping for a second date, know how to express your doubts clearly. Telling them, 'I'll let you know,' might get you away at that moment, but all it will do is have the other person nag you.

Instead, let them know of your doubts. 'I enjoyed your company today, but I'm not sure I want a second date with you.' This statement lets the other person know you do not fancy meeting them again without beating around the bush.

Sure, this second statement will cut through them like a dagger, but they will appreciate your honesty in the future.

And if you like someone, also make this very clear to them. Many people, especially women, will often hinge all their hopes on letting their dates know they want them using subtle hints.

Now, suggestions help convey the message that you like someone, but to avoid doubt, always let the other person know you like them with your words because hints can also be misinterpreted.

So, telling your date, 'I enjoyed your company today and would like to do this again,' communicates to them that you like them and want to see them again.

Clearly stating your position, even when you do not openly say your feelings, helps create a situation with clarity in what will happen. It helps eliminate doubts and assumptions, the two biggest hindrances to effective dating for many of us.

- **Seek Understanding**

A few years ago, as I was scrolling through social media, I came across a post where someone had asked Twitter what to get their partner for their birthday.

I went through the comments and it was a minefield. It was full of the most generalized suggestions ever known to man. I screamed, 'Well, ask them!'

I got frustrated with the fact that this person was asking the internet rather than simply seeking understanding with their partner.

However, I also understand that most of us never grew up in environments with healthy communication. Some people grew up in homes where everyone kept to themselves, so we learned to assume what the others felt rather than speak about it.

And this way of thinking is often solidified once we get to adulthood. It can be hard to change, I understand that.

Nonetheless, to have a thriving relationship, you must get used to the discomfort of seeking understanding from your date or your significant other. Whenever the other person acts a certain way, try to go as deep as possible to find out why.

Maybe you and your ex-partner didn't make an effort to truly understand each other's actions, leaving much unspoken and leading to assumptions. However, it's essential not to repeat this mistake when you start dating again.

Ask your date, 'I feel like you may not be putting as much effort into this relationship as I am. Why is that?' The information you get from questions such as this will provide you with more facts and understanding before making any changes.

Don't immediately turn to social media when your partner's actions puzzle you. Instead, first attempt to communicate and understand your partner by engaging in a conversation. Consider seeking external assistance only if you've genuinely explored all avenues to connect with your partner, and they still seem unresponsive or unreachable.

Furthermore, for best results, always use open-ended questions that make your partner think and respond about how they feel.

When you seek confirmation from your partner regarding your statement, instead of asking, "Do you agree?" try inquiring, "What are your thoughts on what I've said?" The first question typically elicits a simple "yes" or "no" response.

In contrast, the second question is more open-ended, encouraging your partner to express their feelings in greater detail. This fosters a greater sense of openness and clarity in the conversation.

- **Validate Your Partner's Feelings**

It's astonishing how frequently people can be inadvertently dismissive of their partner's emotions. I've come to realize that it's often not intentional.

If, like Alfie, you've caught yourself not truly listening or struggling with effective communication, it can lead to inadvertently dismissing your partner's feelings. It's a common outcome.

When you fail to lend an ear, and your partner brings up an issue later, it's easy to fall into a pattern of dismissal rather than addressing the matter head-on. But it doesn't have to be this way.

Taking the time to acknowledge and validate your partner's feelings is not only a key to more successful dates but, more importantly, to cultivating healthier relationships. People appreciate feeling heard.

While learning to communicate with your new partner, communicating about boundaries is also crucial.

Establishing and Maintaining Boundaries in New Relationships

"You know Tristan, when you get into a relationship with someone, I think some things should be left unsaid. They should just…know." Alfie once said to me during one of our many talks.

I stopped him right there in his tracks.

"No, that is not how relationships work. Trust me, I know about this now more than ever." I replied to him. He looked stunned.

Yet, Alfie's way of thinking is how most people think when they date someone.

Many of us get into relationships without discussing and implementing boundaries. We assume the limits, with the thinking being *'if we are in a relationship, then x or y or z goes without saying.'*

But that isn't it.

Healthy boundaries are a foundation for establishing respect and trust in a relationship. Boundaries indicate your limits and what you are comfortable with at a given time, and it is paramount that your partner or potential partner respects them.

Leaving this crucial part of the relationship up to chance simply because you feel 'they should just know' is how you get off on the wrong foot with someone.

What do I mean? Well, when dating someone new, you need to communicate to them your boundaries at this early stage of a relationship. You might be okay with kissing your date but would not want to go further than that.

You might want to hold hands and hug at home but not be comfortable enough to show affection in public just yet. You might want to meet them publicly rather than at each other's homes until trust is firmly established. These are all examples of boundaries when dating.

Once in a relationship, these boundaries will change. You might agree to be exclusive and no more going on dates with other people. Or it could be that you want to keep your closet all to yourself (for the moment).

But how do you establish them?

- **Understand Yourself First**

Before setting boundaries with someone new, the first course of action is to understand yourself. It would be best to remember that boundaries are lines that you put in place to make yourself comfortable. To set them effectively, you must understand yourself and what makes you comfortable.

For instance, do you enjoy smoking and drinking and wouldn't mind a partner who does the same? Or are you a non-smoker, but a drinker, and wouldn't mind being a smoker?

If so, what do you think of a partner who doesn't do these things? Would you be willing to date them? Are you a religious person? If so, what do you think of dating a partner who isn't religious?

Understanding who you are and what you want in a partner makes it easier to know your boundaries and what is unacceptable.

- **Learn to Communicate Your Boundaries**

This might come as a shock but your partner is not a mind reader.

They will not be able to understand your boundaries just like that. So, it would be best if you let them know about them as soon as you get a hint that the relationship is getting serious. They should know that if the two of you are going to become serious, then there are certain lines that they should respect.

Of course, you don't need to dump all your boundaries on them all at once. Instead, let them know your limits at convenient times.

For example, if your partner is on a date with you but they keep staring at other people, this would be the perfect time to bring up your desire to be exclusive.

Or, if they keep reaching out to touch your belongings, then this would be the best time to bring up the fact that you like it if someone asks first before touching your items.

While at it, remember that your partner also has their boundaries, and you need to pay attention to them too.

Communicating about boundaries early on helps avoid trouble in the future. Even when these boundaries eventually change, the fact that you communicate openly about them will make the transition to the new limits a lot smoother.

- **Learn To Say No**

When dating someone new, there is this overarching desire to please them in every possible way. This desire will often be intense and overcome any other logical feeling you have.

The worst thing about this is that once you have made a new partner comfortable with always being on the receiving end of your good deeds without some boundaries, it is hard to change in the future without putting a strain on the relationship.

Instead, learn early on to say no to demands from your partner that cross your boundaries or make you uncomfortable. Also, remember to tell them no when you don't want to do something. Let your partner know when you are uncomfortable, and don't simply do things to please them. You are only setting yourself up for failure if you do.

Of course, this is not to say that you shouldn't do things for your partner to make them happy. Instead, when you do something for your partner, ensure they reciprocate because relationships all need a little give and take.

- **Speak About Social Media Expectations**

Modern relationships have to contend with social media, and unfortunately, many couples never seem to discuss this boundary, yet it is one of the biggest influences of a modern relationship.

When dating someone new, you both need to discuss what you expect from one another on social media.

Growing up and marrying in an era without social media was fortunate for many of us. However, for those of you who have dated after a divorce, social media may have become an issue in your relationships.

One of the most significant issues when it comes to social media is interacting with other people, especially those who may pose a risk to your relationship. In other words, this means how your girlfriend interacts with other men online or how your boyfriend interacts with women online. Same sex couples are also not immune to this!

Both of you need to discuss what is acceptable and what isn't. Don't make assumptions.

The same is true for posting images on social media. What would the both of you be comfortable with? How would you compromise if you are not on the same page about it?

For example, does having a partner who posts photos in revealing attire bother you? Would you be okay with your partner knowing your social media passwords? Would you like your partner to post you on their social media?

These discussions help you establish what you are comfortable with and what you aren't so that you are aware of each other's preferences. Once again, I reiterate that the boundaries will be for you, and not to control your partner.

So, if you aren't comfortable with a partner who posts suggestive photos of themselves on social media, rather than say, 'You should stop posting these photos,' tell them, 'I am not comfortable with you posting these photos. How should we go about this?'

In the second sentence, you have established a boundary you wouldn't like crossed without coming off as controlling, which is what the first statement is.

- **Discuss Financial Boundaries**

Ah, money! The most exciting part of a relationship, amiright!

Joking aside, if you and your date feel that the relationship is getting serious, discussing money should be up in your boundary discussions.

It's shocking just how many people are in long-term relationships and have never discussed financial boundaries with their partners. Yet, many feel resentful of their partner due to the partner crossing financial boundaries.

One person I met was being driven mad by their partner's excessive spending, lack of financial discipline, and disregard for money. And you want to know how long they have been married? Ten years. It was a mess because how do you try to bring up financial boundaries after this long!

According to divorce statistics, finances are one of the biggest causes of divorce, ranking higher than infidelity.

Consequently, establishing financial boundaries early in a relationship can help you avoid future stress if things get serious.

Consider talking about your financial budget before going out on a date. Ensure you and your date agree about the best place to eat that won't dent your pockets. Discuss who will pay and how you would go about paying.

Conversely, discuss how you would sort out finances together when things get serious. Things like, are you comfortable borrowing money from each other? Should you borrow money from each other? What are the expectations around repayments?

Remember not to hesitate to say no if your partner borrows too much at your expense. Additionally, if you have a general rule against loaning money to your partner, let them know early. This will help reset their expectations and let them know whether that is something they can live with or not.

- **Personal Space Boundaries**

Once in a relationship, many couples often fuse their spaces such that it becomes harder to tell who owns what. Now, this is not necessarily a bad thing.

When both parties are on the same page about it, it can be pretty sweet. However, discuss early on where personal space boundaries begin and end. It would help if you said what you are comfortable sharing and what you aren't.

You might have no problem with my partner wearing my shirts or hoodies, but you might not want to share a towel or personal effects. You might also not like sharing an intimate item (like a toothbrush!) without being asked first.

Some people might even enjoy sleeping in their own beds from time to time. Whatever constitutes your personal space, let your partner know early on so that they decide whether they are comfortable with that agreement or not.

You can discuss how you would compromise on it, but at the end of the day, both of you need to be aware of how you interpret personal space. Nonetheless, you shouldn't compromise your personal space so much that you become uncomfortable with the arrangement.

Communicating your needs and establishing your boundaries early in the relationship helps start the relationship on a sound footing. Additionally, when you share openly with someone, it opens the path to vulnerability and building trust.

Chapter 5: Embracing Vulnerability and Trust

'Don't get too attached; people leave,' 'Always be ready for your partner to hurt you.' I am pretty sure you have read this more than once on social media.

Welcome to the age of mindless cynicism.

At face value, these sentiments seem like sound advice, but only if you want to live a life of casual flings and no serious long-term relationship (I'm not judging you).

However, if you want to get into another serious, committed relationship, then you will need to learn or re-learn to be vulnerable and trust your partner wholly.

Vulnerability[xv] is one of the things that make long-term relationships seem scary to some people, especially after a heartbreak.

It is understandable not to want to be open to anyone again after getting your heart shattered, but you should not live a life of fear and skepticism because there is still a lot of love for you to give and receive.

Embracing Vulnerability as a Strength in Dating

Picture this; you are coming off a long-term relationship and are meeting someone else who is, let's say a divorcee.

Now, you are still discovering yourself after the heartbreak and your date also seems to not be completely over his/her ended marriage.

Due to a lack of trust between the two of you, you end up talking more about something trivial like the Kardashians because both of you have cold feet about opening up to each other. And, as a result, both of you leave that date unsatisfied and full of regret.

If you have been on a date like this, then understand that you need to open yourself up to being vulnerable and to trust so that you can enjoy your dates.

But, why is vulnerability significant in dating? you ask. Well, because:

- **It Deepens Your Bond**

When you can openly share both the good and the bad in your life and turn to someone at your worst, and they hold you and soothe you, you feel a profound closeness with that person.

This is what vulnerability does in dating. It allows you and the other person to understand each other deeper, making you grow close and become each other's pillar of strength.

This closeness helps establish a stronger bond as you both open up to each other deeply.

- **It Encourages Self-Regulation**

Being vulnerable with someone involves going through things that are typically uncomfortable. Asserting your needs, establishing boundaries, and revealing insecurity are parts of embracing vulnerability.

When you find someone who doesn't judge you and makes you feel at home in their presence, it becomes easier to do these things, which then helps you learn how to regulate and cope with the uncomfortable emotions that come with your insecurities or asserting yourself.

You will no longer be weighed down by your insecurities or have a problem asserting your needs because you have found someone who listens to you and validates your feelings.

- **Builds Emotional Resilience**

Sometimes, dating can have a rollercoaster of emotions, but vulnerability helps strengthen emotional resilience.

Being open about your vulnerabilities and feelings teaches you to handle uncertainty, disappointment, and rejection better. This is because vulnerability enables you to realize that your self-worth depends not on validation from others but on how you understand your values.

This strong character built by vulnerability becomes a guide to help you navigate the downs and ups of dating with self-assurance and grace.

- **Helps Reduce Conflict**

Many couples who frequently clash often have one thing in common – they will be driven by ego, which is the antithesis of vulnerability.

One man I met said to me, without blinking, *'I always have the last word in an argument with people I date."*

You might judge this man but many of us are like him. In arguments, we aim more to win than resolve conflict.

However, when you embrace vulnerability, you will find it easier to resolve conflicts without ego.

You see, when you feel as though you cannot express yourself without judgment, you do not feel listened to, and your partner is dismissive of how you think, that creates fertile grounds for conflict.

However, when you and your partner embrace vulnerability, you communicate openly, easing tension and conflict. Exposure comes with closeness, intimacy, and accountability.

All of these come about due to open and honest dialogue, the foundation on which vulnerability is built. With the path of communication wide open, it reduces chances of destructive conflict behaviour like avoidance, deflection, blaming, and shouting.

But how do you build vulnerability, you may ask? Well, let us look at that:

How To Build Vulnerability

- **Start Small**

When Roger goes on dates, he prefers to mention his divorce early on to avoid any surprises later. How the other person reacts to this information helps Roger decide whether to share more about himself or take things slowly.

In your case, consider sharing something relatively minor about yourself that not many people know. For instance, if you have a small insecurity, share it with your date and observe their response. This can provide valuable insights into your potential compatibility.

Are they supportive? Or are they dismissive? If they show support, that is a positive sign to continue opening up to them. If they are dismissive, cut ties immediately.

- **Express Your Feelings**

Sharing feelings also builds vulnerability. Never get tired of letting your partner know that you love and cherish them.

Nonetheless, also let them know when they've hurt you. Being open with how you both feel helps you understand each other better and do better, building a deeper connection.

- **Be Your Partner's Safe Space**

Oh, the joy of knowing that your partner will be there for you during the toughest of times!

Becoming someone that your partner turns to when they feel at their worst is only possible through vulnerability.

Vulnerability is the glue that holds intimate relationships together; it makes couples know each other so well that they seem almost like they are telepathically linked.

Vulnerability gives us that tingling sensation whenever we look at a couple and marvel at how well they get along.

Building Trust in Yourself and Others After a Breakup

'How could I have been so stupid?'

I can't tell you how many times I've heard this statement from people after a breakup.

The desire to blame yourself will often be great during this time of pain and trust in yourself and others will often hit an all-time low. I understand you when you begin to believe that you will always make the wrong choices.

However, that is not true. You won't always make the wrong choices and here is how to make it possible to make the right choices. Here is how to learn how to trust yourself and others again.

- **Take Control**

The desire to become a sitting duck after a breakup and just wait on fate is strong, but you need to have a stronger will if you are to regain trust in yourself again.

Your trust in yourself is directly related to your actions. So, rather than sitting around and waiting for something, take control of the situation. Take up projects at work that will have you believing in yourself again.

I started writing as a way to get over my heartbreak but I soon realized that it opened me up to learning more about myself, and my abilities. Just a simple action led to me completely transforming my life for the better.

When you become proactive in your life, you learn how to trust in your actions, your ability to make the right choices, and your ability to heal.

- **Avoid Bad Habits**

During recovery, some people may turn to habits like drinking or smoking to cope with heartbreak. This pattern is not uncommon, as I've observed in friends. However, these habits tend to exacerbate their emotional struggles rather than provide genuine relief.

It is evident that instead of facilitating coping, adopting such detrimental habits can impede the process of rebuilding trust within oneself. These behaviours often lead to increased self-doubt, undermining one's confidence in handling the situation.

In situations like these, it's advisable to seek out healthy coping mechanisms that foster self-belief.

Engaging in new hobbies, acquiring fresh skills, or exploring activities that offer long-term fulfilment are more constructive alternatives than temporary pleasures that ultimately leave you feeling worse off.

- **Give Yourself Space And Time**

Taking time for yourself after a breakup is not only okay but essential. It's a chance to rediscover who you are, heal, and grow.

Rushing into dating too soon may hinder your personal growth and lead to poor dating choices. Give yourself the space and time you deserve to rebuild and emerge even stronger before diving back into the dating world.

Remember, it took Alfie over a year before he even contemplated dating again so know that you do not need to rush into things.

This is normal, and you shouldn't feel like you are failing.

- **Learn To Communicate Effectively**

Oops, the C word makes another appearance.

The truth is that trust is not founded on assumptions. As you continually learn to rebuild trust in the other person, communicate your expectations effectively and clearly. Let the other person know what you have or have not committed to.

Building trust with other people is a risk, and thus, it involves both you and others taking chances to prove trustworthiness, which will only happen effectively through communication.

Communication will also help you weed out people who are untrustworthy, rather than walking around believing that everyone is dishonest, which can make navigating the dating world difficult.

- **Take Your Time**

It can take even months to fully trust someone and that being so, understanding this means that you should be patient.

I have gone on dates with people whom it took weeks to open up fully to. For others, it took even months. However, in none of these situations did I ever trust someone after just a few hours or days.

The first steps towards building trust should be small and need small commitments. For instance, you might not invite your date to your home after just a few initial outings. That is a significant step and needs a lot of commitment.

However, you could learn to establish trust with them by lending them items and establishing their trustworthiness before moving on to more significant obligations.

- **Keep An Open Mind When Dating**

And finally, to learn to trust, and keep an open mind when meeting new people, give a clean slate to every date that you meet and avoid judging people before you know them.

Building trust, whether with yourself or the people around you, requires a lot of patience. It is also an ongoing process, which means that commitment is needed.

Like how laying the foundation of a building will often take a lot of work, so too is building trust and embracing vulnerability. So, don't be too hard on yourself. Enjoy the process of dating as much as possible and before you know it, you are back to trusting yourself and your dates again.

Chapter 6: Overcoming Dating Anxiety

In an ordinary scenario, dating is already an anxiety-inducing situation so dating with a broken heart is going to be twice as anxiety-inducing.

Imagine waking up in the morning, feeling great about yourself because you finally met someone whom you vibe with and are going to meet for the first time.

Perhaps you met through a dating app and have been chatting and now you will be meeting in person for the first time.

But then – it hits you. That wave of sorrow, of sadness, that shattering feeling of your previous heartbreak. You go from confident and happy to a blabbering mess because you just cannot bring yourself to forget the past.

If this is you, I understand you. Dating after a breakup is tough. The thought of putting yourself out there knowing that the chances of another heartbreak are 50/50 is enough to send anyone recoiling back to their shell.

But if you wanted to recoil back to your shell, then you wouldn't be here. You are here because you want to overcome the anxiety, put yourself out there, and enjoy dating again.

So what do you do?

Managing Anxiety and Fears Associated with Dating

When you feel dating anxiety, learning to manage and cope with it, rather than trying to resist it, will see you through.

Here, then is how to manage dating anxiety and fears.

- **Surround Yourself With Emotionally Safe People**

If you find yourself in a situation where you are feeling overwhelmed with dating anxiety, then I suggest you put emotionally safe people around you.

I cannot overstress the importance of having people with whom you can be vulnerable with around.

I've seen people who were completely unable to overcome their initial dating anxiety turn into confident companion simply because they found someone to help them find their feet again.

So, find a friend, a family member - maybe even a parent or sibling, who will be your emotional anchor. Share your fears with them, and in turn, they will give you that encouragement you need to get back to the dating scene.

For example, your confidant could help you practice communicating when out on a date, which can take some edge off your fears since their help can give you an idea of how to carry yourself on a date.

You wouldn't need to follow their advice or guide as stated, but just their structure can give you more confidence when out on a date.

- **Be More Open And Honest About Yourself**

Research in 2016 found that self-disclosure helps alleviate social anxiety and helps increase the desire to connect again. Self-disclosure means simply being open and honest about yourself to the other person.

I know that it seems counterintuitive as you will often feel less inclined to share when anxious, but learning to be honest about yourself makes you very comfortable around people

First, being honest about yourself makes you feel a lot more comfortable with the other person, easing the anxiety. It is also the first step towards establishing trust and building a connection.

Of course, when you are being open about yourself, don't share your deepest secrets with this stranger. Be honest about your interests, intentions, desires, and such, and not about family issues or previous trauma (These things should be reserved for when you are already serious with that person).

The openness and honesty about relatively minor things can help you feel more relaxed with your date, even as you gauge their trustworthiness.

- **Understand Your Values And Needs**

Now that you are recovering from a heartbreak, what do you seek in a partner? What are your goals, values, and needs in life?

What would you wish a potential partner to embody?

You see, anxiety in dating also comes from not knowing what you want.

There was this person that I worked with who would often list down things that he wanted in a potential partner. Now, his criteria often changed from time to time, but he was confident in himself and what he wanted.

"To be honest, Tristan, it's because I've been hurt before, and having a list like this not only helps me go on dates with people I want, it also helps me feel less anxious since I don't waste my time trying to impress people I don't align with."

This point is what got me thinking and I learned that he was right.

When you have an idea of your values, you become less anxious because you have solid grounds to stand on when dating. Much of the dating anxiety will often come from feelings of the unknown, of not knowing what will come next.

However, when you establish your values and needs, you have a rough idea of what you want to go next, and you will act in ways that will lead you in that direction, which helps ease your fears as you feel more in control.

- **Be Nonjudgmental To Yourself**

'I am scared of dating. That makes me such a loser.' You might whisper to yourself whenever you experience dating anxiety.

Unfortunately, saying such things to yourself will only make you feel worse. You don't overcome dating anxiety by shaming yourself.

Shaming yourself makes you more anxious because it simply highlights the flaw. Instead, practice being compassionate with yourself.

When you look at yourself and your actions nonjudgmentally, you create perfect conditions to understand yourself better, thus creating practical solutions to working on that.

So, instead of shaming yourself for anxiety, sit back and think, 'I feel anxious and scared about dating. This is perfectly normal, and I am not a loser for it. But why do I feel this way?'

Slow down and acknowledge how you feel, then try to get to the root of it. Are you anxious because you still feel attached to your ex? Are you nervous because you still hold onto the hurtful things your ex said? Or are you anxious simply because you do not wish to put yourself in a vulnerable position again?

When you are compassionate to yourself, you understand yourself better and create better conditions to get to the root cause of the anxiety and deal with it.

- **Plan Your Dates Accordingly**

One of the worst things that you can do is jump right into dates, especially when recovering from a heartbreak. You will find yourself stuttering, lacking confidence, and unable to speak, simply because you aren't ready.

So, take your time when re-entering the dating scene.

Since anxiety often stems from the fear of the unknown, it makes sense to plan meticulously for each date. When meeting someone, gather as much information as possible: the date details, location, time, directions, planned activities, and more.

This level of preparation helps create a sense of predictability and control, which can be incredibly calming.

Even if you're not the one planning the date, it's advisable not to leave everything to your partner if you're dealing with dating anxiety. Politely express your preferences and let your date know that you would appreciate having all necessary information shared with you before the big day arrives.

- **Remember, Your Date Is Also Anxious**

This is one of my go-to techniques when dealing with dating anxiety. I often sit down and as I feel the anxiety rising, I remind myself,

"My date is also just as nervous as I am."

Believe it or not, it helps me calm down and it will also help you.

By knowing that your date is also anxious, it helps you humanize them rather than put them on a pedestal, which is what most of us do with people we like.

Then, when you meet your date, you can break the ice by admitting that you feel nervous, and then jokingly asking them if they feel it too. 'Getting here was hectic. I couldn't tie my shoelaces because I was trembling and nervous. I think you feel it too, am I right?'

Even if they don't admit to feeling nervous, you have already created perfect conversational conditions, enabling you to be comfortable with each other.

As you manage your anxiety, you must practice self-care and build resilience to cope better in the dating scene.

- **Practicing Self-care and Building Resilience**

As you try to get back to dating, ensure that you care for yourself and build your emotional resilience so that you don't take inevitable setbacks to heart.

Strength shows its true mettle when confronted with trauma, tragedy, adversity, or threats. Going through a breakup, especially one involving a long-term partner, is a profoundly challenging experience for many of us, often leaving us feeling defeated.

However, it's crucial to recognize that it doesn't have to define us. You have the capacity and willpower to overcome this.

Here's a guide on fostering resilience and practicing self-care within yourself.

- **Take a Break**

I know you will be itching to return to the dating scene as soon as you feel healed, but I suggest you take a more extended break from dating.

Taking a break from dating lets you exist within yourself. It becomes a way to reconnect with yourself without the extension of a romantic partner.

By taking a break entirely from dating, even after you feel healed, you are helping create a strong self-identity that will come in handy in case of future heartbreak.

I can confidently tell you that after my divorce and that long break I took from dating, I got a firm idea of who I was - and this new me will handle any future heartbreak a lot better than my past self would.

- **Care For Your Physical Health**

Well, we cannot talk about self-care without talking about physical care. Look at yourself in the mirror. Think of how much of your physical self is wasting away due to the pain of heartbreak.

You wouldn't want a lack of confidence in your physical self to get in the way of you dating again. So, get up and begin working on your body!

Below are some ways to care for your physical health:

Eat a healthy balanced diet: Eating healthy food is the first and most critical way to care for yourself. Eat a balanced meal daily to give your body a fighting chance if you get into another stressful event.

Physical fitness: Regular exercise will make you physically fit but, most importantly, help you feel good about yourself.

Dress well: Practice proper personal and environmental hygiene, wear clean and fitting clothes, and ensure your hair is neat. You will be surprised at how ready you feel to tackle anything that comes your way.

The above ways of caring for yourself provide a solid base to build resilience because they give you a sense of accomplishment and confidence, two things you need to bounce back.

- **Practice Emotional Self-Care**

The emotional turmoil following a heartbreak and trying to date again is enough to send anyone into a spiral.

One of my close friends, recently divorced, told me that it felt as though someone was carving his heart open with a scalpel and planting stinging nettle on the wound.

Ouch!

So, to help yourself recover and overcome any anxiety, acknowledge your emotions and learn to deal with them.

Connect with loved ones and nurture your soul through things that make you happy. You might be asking how this makes you resilient. Well, it is because, as you engage in activities that bring you joy, you will also learn how to handle the negative emotions that come with it.

For example, you enjoy swimming and feel joy each time. But how do you self-regulate? How do you handle those days you don't want it as much?

Through connecting with your positive emotions, you also learn how to deal with the consequent negative emotion, which can come in handy when you are feeling down, for example, from a heartbreak, which is the direct opposite feeling of the romantic love that preceded it.

- **Don't Forget Your Mental Stimulation**

Ah, the power of the mind!

In recovering from heartbreak, learn to do activities that maintain your mental cognitive abilities.

When recovering from a heartbreak, and wanting to get back to the dating scene, building resilience will be one of the ways to reduce anxiety.

Of course, any of the activities mentioned in the previous sections can be considered mentally stimulating, but to build resilience, focus on exercises that specifically target your mind—reading, solving puzzles, and learning something new all help to teach you how to stay the course and see something through.

Maintaining our cognitive abilities gives us a fighting chance when encountering a mentally challenging situation, such as heartbreak. Of course, this is not to say that you won't feel the pain of heartbreak (Of course you will), but it means that you will have better coping strategies due to the previous lessons you learned from stimulating your mind.

- **Practice Having A Positive Mindset**

Oh, the folly of youth! Being carefree and optimistic and positive without a care in the world.

Well, you can also try to reconnect with that part of you after recovering from a heartbreak and experiencing dating anxiety.

I understand that it's hard to be positive when you are feeling like the weight of the world is on your shoulders, but I suggest you just push on with it.

Shift your perspective to more positive parts of dating so that you don't focus on the negative and develop cold feet

- **Learn To Have Problem-Solving Skills**

Dating, as you will come to realize is nothing but learning how to live with others and solve problems together.

Thus, getting a head start and putting yourself in the driving seat of problem-solving will ease any tension in your body.

For example, during conflicts, rather than seeing it as a sign that your budding relationship is on the rocks, you can use this as an opportunity for you and your partner to solidify the relationship further.

This means that you should look into alternative ways of conflict resolution besides shouting, like resting on the issue until both of you are emotionally ready to solve it.

- **Be Flexible And Adaptable**

Most importantly, be flexible and adaptable if you are to enjoy dating.

Be free and open to new experiences with your date. Turn that anxiety you feel into a fire in your belly to face your fears.

You will be pleasantly shocked to learn that when you are flexible and adaptable, dating becomes much more enjoyable.

Readiness, Rejection, and Retreating into Yourself

I wish I could tell you that once you've healed there won't be any more pain, that there would be no more rejection.

The sad reality though, is that rejection will always be a distinct possibility.

Rejection is part of dating: There is no escaping this one. When you put yourself out there to date, you also put yourself up for rejection.

This is not meant to discourage you, but quite the opposite – it is meant to make you realize that dating has risks, among them being rejection, and thus, you need to be comfortable with that risk to have any success in the field.

Besides, you will also be the one doing the rejection sometimes, so someone rejecting you wouldn't mean that they are a terrible person or malicious; in the same way, I believe you wouldn't leave someone simply out of malice.

Avoiding dating isn't solving anything: I have no problem if you stay away from dating as a personal principle.

However, if you decide not to date simply because you are anxious but still long for that romantic love, you are setting yourself up for a life full of regret and heartbreak.

Yes, when you decide not to date simply because you are too scared, you will still end up breaking your heart. So, what would you instead do – put yourself out there, risk heartbreak but find your perfect love, or retreat into yourself, long for dating but end up heartbroken anyway due to regret with no chance at love?

Dating is all about action: Movies and other TV shows have created this idea in many people that your perfect match will find you, and you will fall in love instantly without even trying.

But as one of my friends put it, "If you want mashed potato and steak, you get off the couch and make some mashed potato and steak!"

Dating is mashed potato and steak. Delicious but more importantly, need work. And even when you do not put in action or work, you are still acting, only that your inaction leads you away from meeting your potential match.

So, even when you meet someone and instantly become fascinated, you must try to learn more about each other. There is nothing natural about love finding you and working out without effort. It would help if you were willing to take action in dating to find your perfect match.

Dating anxiety should not be what stands between you and your perfect match. You can easily overcome it by understanding yourself, being patient with yourself, and not overthinking.

Even during a heartbreak, practicing self-care and resilience can help you quickly recover and overcome any anxiety you experience. All in all, always ensure that your actions are leading you toward your perfect match, not away. And as you seek your partner, be ready to pick up on any red flags.

Chapter 7: Red Flags and Healthy Relationship Dynamics

Ah, red flags. How many times have you heard of this word? I bet you may have lost count because it is a word that is thrown around quite a lot these days.

Here is something to do. Just open up any social media app, and search for the word red flags. See what comes up.

I know that many of you are familiar with the word, and heck, after a breakup, that is probably all that you think about.

But what are the red flags?

Unfortunately, the term red flags can be taken out of context on the internet, leading to a washing down of the word's meaning.

Let's say you meet someone new. This person seems to be the person of your dreams. They are attractive, and you two get along very well. However, you notice that they have some characteristics that are concerning to you.

They may show excessive control early on, or begin to try and dictate your life. Perhaps they say things that no normal person would say, and persistently say these things. Perhaps they send passive aggressive texts when you say you can't meet tonight for dinner?

When someone displays such persistent problematic behaviour, then that is considered a red flag.

So, we can define red flags as a series of behaviours in a person, which might indicate that the person might be toxic, abusive, or manipulative. These behaviours that someone displays early on when you meet them act as a warning about the toxic person they are.

So, red flags[xvi] are more than human flaws. For example, when someone says something wrong simply because of social anxiety, which is a normal human flaw, especially if they show awareness and try not to do it, then this is not necessarily a red flag.

For a behaviour to be a red flag, it has to be a negative, persistent, and problematic behaviour that may be a hint at a deeper problem.

By becoming aware of these common red flags, you can avoid becoming involved with someone toxic.

Recognizing Warning Signs and Red Flags in Potential Partners

Recognizing red flags in potential partners is crucial as it helps you steer clear of individuals who could pose significant risks. Here are some common red flags to watch out for in people.

- **Very Controlling Behaviour**

So, you've met your cute date and they seem nice enough. However, as the date goes on, they begin to tell you what to do. At first, it seems innocent, but then, they become increasingly obsessed with what and how you should do things.

Now, that is a red flag! Sit up and take notice.

Usually, early on, controlling behaviour will seem innocent. Perhaps they might ask you to dress or wear things a certain way. Then as the two of you continue dating, they might ask you to speak to them in a certain way.

Then, before you know it, they might begin requesting you to stop communicating with certain friends or family. Now, wait a minute! That is not normal, is it?

No, it's not. Someone who wants to dictate your life is displaying early signs of being an abuser. They aren't setting boundaries. *They are trying to control you.*

- **Emotional Dysregulation**

So, your date has just had their order mixed up. I mean these things happen right? All they have to do is call over the waiter and let them know of the mistake, right?

What, no? They just shot up from their seat and rushed into the kitchen. They are livid and out of control. You try to calm them down, but they are out of control. It requires three security guards to get them restrained.

That is what emotional dysregulation is. We all get inconvenienced from time to time, but if someone displays a lack of inhibition, that is a huge red flag.

Emotional dysregulation means that if this person is your partner, you will receive the strongest of their emotions, especially the negative ones. When they get angry, they could insult you or even get physical.

If they are sad, they might completely shut you out, or if they feel you have wronged them, they might become highly passive-aggressive.

Emotional dysregulation means you will never be able to solve issues with them since they will not have the emotional capacity to sit through their feelings and work through them.

So, if your potential partner gets extremely angry that they lash out and ruin everyone's day just because the server got their order wrong, that is a red flag.

Sure, the waiter getting your order wrong is frustrating, but most emotionally functional people will understand that it is an honest mistake and ask for a change. What they won't do is insult the waiter, or the restaurant and spend the whole date angry.

- **Lack of Principles**

Have you ever met someone who just has no stand? I'm talking about people whose entire shtick is 'This is the trend so let me do it'.

Such people will often have no values and will spout the opinion that is acceptable at the time.

Let's start by acknowledging that as social beings, we all desire acceptance. Consequently, we often make an effort to comprehend the beliefs of others, and at times, we may even adopt them ourselves.

However, even as we do this, we will constantly maintain our core values, and a sense of self, because our identity matters most to us. Even if we change, we change based on our evolving beliefs, not simply because someone else says so.

People who switch up their values and beliefs at the flip of a coin will never make great partners because they will never know what they want.

These people will try to tailor your relationship to other people's; they will try to make you be like someone else and will have no problems cheating on you because their friend said so and such.

A lack of principles will also come with a lack of boundaries and lack of emotional concern, meaning that you bear the emotional burden of the relationship alone.

- **Lack of Trust**

I wouldn't expect you to trust your date right off the bat. Skepticism early on during dating is normal and healthy!

But have you ever met someone who just treats you with suspicion right away?

A friend of mine once mentioned to me a date they went on. It was their first date. However, the date asked my friend to put her phone on the table (they both put the phones on the table).

My friend then noticed that the date kept staring at my friend's phone.

"It's hard to believe that someone like you doesn't get calls all the time," the date said. My friend thought it was a joke and just laughed it off.

But the date was dead serious.

"What are you hiding from me?" The date asked, his tone more menacing.

It was then that my friend realized they were serious. My friend quickly left the date and blocked their number!

Such a display of lack of trust is not normal. That was their first date and already the other person was showing that they didn't trust my friend.

So, if you find yourself on a date with someone who shows early on that they don't believe you in any way, that's a red flag.

- **Selfish Behaviour**

Allow me to just state off the bat that a little selfishness is expected. We are all self-centered to a certain extent.

However, we also know when to stop being self-centered and show interest in other people.

I know you've been on a date where you got so excited talking about yourself that you did not give time for your date to speak. Then, you recognized it and excused yourself, apologized, and asked your date to speak.

That is not selfishness as a red flag.

What I am talking about is your date going on and on and on about themselves without a single bother about you. They show no interest in you or your needs. Only them and their needs seem to matter.

It is when your date goes on and on about themselves not out of excitement or nervousness but rather, due to self-absorption.

For example, when organizing the date, they might often choose convenient locations, even if they know it is inconvenient for you. Or they could try to downplay your achievements or accomplishments by mentioning their own actions as if it's a competition.

Someone who consistently fails to humble themselves may exhibit traits of narcissism. So, if they appear uncaring about your needs, even after you've pointed out a minor oversight, it's essential to remain vigilant.

- **Watch How They Talk About Their Exes**

Have you ever been on a date with people who go on and on about how wrong their ex was? Such people will often tell anyone who listens just how bad their ex was.

They will badmouth their exes, and speak about them in such derogatory terms that you wonder if they had ever truly liked them.

Do you know such people? Yeah. Well never give someone who does this a second date. Run for the hills!

A well-adjusted person should maintain some level of respect for someone that they once loved and cared about. They should also take responsibility for their role in how the previous relationship ended.

Red flags are guiding signs that help us understand how to proceed and even how to cut things off. Now, I will say this, before cutting things off with someone displaying these red flags, bring up the issue with them first.

Tell them how their behavior is making you reconsider the relationship. It might be that someone is unaware of that part about themselves.

By letting them know, you allow them to correct their ways. If someone fails to correct their ways after you bring it up to them, that is yet another red flag. Run as fast as you can.

However, even as you look out for red flags, there are also signs that you should look out for that indicate healthy relationship dynamics.

Nurturing Healthy Relationship Dynamics Based on Respect and Compatibility

I know your favourite romantic comedies make it seem like normal relationships are fairy tales between two unlikely people making it work. Unfortunately, reality is a bit different.

Unlike what pop culture art might tell you, healthy relationships are built on intentionality and compatibility, not limerence or infatuation. Healthy relationships are founded on practicality and compatibility.

• Have Realistic Expectations

Wow! I remember the first time I fell in love. It felt as though something magical from heaven had fallen into my heart.

This feeling of infatuation and limerence felt great and it led me to believe that the object of my affection was this perfect being who would come into my life and make it better with no problems.

I know you have also felt the same about someone too. Well, allow for those feelings of limerence to fade. Allow yourself to get to know this person; both their good and their flaws.

This way, you recalibrate expectations and approach the other person with a realistic view of who they are and how things could evolve.

• Talk With Each Other

Sticking with infatuation and limerence, I don't know if you've ever noticed but whenever you have a huge crush on someone, you often never enjoy talking to them – at least as much as you thought you would.

Well, that's infatuation for you. In infatuation, you will often be more in love with the idea of the person, rather than the person. This is why communicating with them often feels underwhelming – because they don't match the idea you have of them.

To nurture a healthy relationship then, you need to learn how to communicate with the object of your affection.

It is through communicating with the other person that compatibility or incompatibility is discovered. When you talk, you will quickly gain insight into whether your prospective relationship can work or not. You will understand whether your values and beliefs are compatible or not.

Simply starting a relationship based on your physical attraction to each other creates a recipe for disaster. Even if both of you do not intend for the relationship to be serious, you will still need to communicate this to keep expectations in check.

- **Be Willing To Compromise**

This one time I was at a social gathering and the topic of conversation inevitably went into relationships.

Most of our conversations were productive and educational. However, it was when one of the people there blurted something out that the mood changed.

***"It's either you get me as I am, or walk*,"** this person said.

I asked them how long their previous relationship was. They said three years but they hadn't been in a serious relationship in close to seven years.

Then it all made sense to me.

You see, if you also reason like this person, you might think you are setting a boundary through such a stance - but that is a toxic lack of compromise on your part.

You and the other party need to be willing to compromise to have a healthy relationship. Now compromises need to come from both parties to reflect a healthy relationship.

For example, let us say your partner prefers never to share any of their items. On the other hand, you are free and don't mind sharing most of your things.

That is an unhealthy relationship dynamic if your partner always shares your things but doesn't let you share theirs. You are at a disadvantage because your compromise is not reciprocated.

A healthy settlement would be sharing your items with your partner and agreeing to share specific things with you.

- **Be Dependable**

Normal relationships are predictable.

After a heartbreak, your idea of what constitutes a good relationship might have changed but always remember that a good partner is dependable.

Dependability also involves taking responsibility. When you wrong your partner, admit your mistake and correct where you went wrong.

Hold up your end of the bargain as you promised, and your partner does the same. Dependability helps solidify the trust that the two of you have already established, making your bond more robust and secure.

- **Always Show Gratitude**

One of my friends has been in a happy marriage for over three decades. I once asked him how they managed to do it and he sat up, looked straight at me, and said,

"My partner and I often never forget to say 'thank you' to each other even for the smallest of gestures."

That was an eye-opening moment because it made me realize that long-term relationships are founded on **appreciating the little things** that your partner does.

When you and your partner make each other feel appreciated, you further improve the dynamics of your relationship. While at it, say 'thank you' to them after acts of kindness they extend your way.

- **Provide Them With Emotional Support**

This same friend who opened my eyes to gratitude also told me,

"You need to be the first person that your partner thinks of when they are happy, sad, distressed, or feeling anything."

Being an emotional pillar for your partner means that you validate their feelings. Listen to them when they express their feelings. Validate their feelings by acting on what they said.

Give them compliments at every opportunity, and ensure that you are intentional with each praise so that it doesn't come off as if you are checking it off a list. Each compliment should be specific to a given context.

And each day, ask them how they are doing and listen actively to what they say. Hug them even if you cannot offer them a solution to a given problem. The hug lets them know they are not alone in whatever they are going through.

- **Learn To Forgive**

I once heard someone say that marriage is nothing but a series of apologies and forgiveness.

I don't agree with the sentiment in totality but I get the gist of it. Living with someone in close proximity for years will inevitably result in the two of you stepping on each other's toes.

Learning how to apologize and seek forgiveness is crucial because much of the friction will be on what could be considered 'small issues'. By apologizing and forgiving these minor issues, you stop them from becoming any worse in the future.

Now, the reason I did not agree with the sentiment completely is because, on the other hand, if you are constantly apologizing, forgiving, or seeking forgiveness, then that could be a sign of trouble.

Healthy relationships are built on trust, reliability, communication, and every once in a while, forgiveness. And all these are established during the dating phase so if the signs are not positive at the start, don't sit around hoping for change.

Chapter 8: Exploring Diverse Relationships and Orientations

In the modern dating world, diversity and inclusivity are not just buzzwords; they're a reality. The landscape of love has evolved significantly over the years, now embracing all different sexual orientations and relationship structures. It's no longer simply about man meets woman; it's about human meets human, heart connects with heart.

Just as our taste buds vary, so does human sexuality.

Take Robert and Mary, for example. They first crossed paths in the year 2000 while working together and gradually fell in love during their shared lunch breaks. Their journey led them to marriage, and they spent many years together.

Now, fast forward more than two decades, and as they step into the dating world once again, they find themselves encountering a plethora of new relationship dynamics and types they may not have previously encountered.

Much like Robert and Mary, many of you might be emerging from or seeking a heterosexual, monogamous relationship. However, as I've discovered through my own recent dating experiences, you may also notice that people are increasingly embracing diverse sexual orientations and gender identities in the dating landscape.

And guess what? That's perfectly normal! Science supports this idea with studies showing that sexual orientation exists on a spectrum rather than binary terms (straight or gay).

I've met several people, particularly online, and as I got to know them, they have openly admitted that they are in fact already married and their partner knows/accepts that they are seeing other people occasionally. Some couples also like to 'play' together with their partner and another person – irrespective of their gender.

I'm sharing this with you, not to put you off online dating, but just so that you are aware you may come across all different types of relationship models while you are looking for a new partner.

You too may find that many people have 'open relationship' or 'ethically non-monogamous' listed as their relationship status.

This shift towards acceptance and understanding allows for more authentic connections as people feel free to express who they truly are without fear of judgment or rejection.

But what does this mean for you, stepping back into the dating scene after a divorce? It means a world filled with opportunities to explore new experiences and broaden your horizons.

As you embark on this journey, it's important to approach it with an open mind. You might meet someone who identifies as bisexual or someone who prefers non-monogamous relationships. These realities may be new to you but remember that at its core, every relationship is about mutual respect, trust, understanding and love.

As you embark on this exploration of diverse relationships and orientations in the post-divorce dating world, consider the following guidelines to ensure you navigate this landscape with grace and respect:

1. **Open Communication**: Honest and open communication is the foundation of any successful relationship. Be willing to discuss your expectations, desires, and boundaries with potential partners, and

encourage them to do the same. This creates an environment of trust and understanding.

2. **Education and Empathy**: Take the time to educate yourself about different sexual orientations and relationship structures. Seek to understand the experiences and challenges that individuals with diverse identities may face. Empathy and acceptance go a long way in forming meaningful connections.

3. **Respect Individual Choices**: Remember that everyone's journey is unique. If you encounter someone who identifies with a different sexual orientation or relationship style, respect their choices and preferences. Avoid making assumptions or passing judgment.

4. **Stay True to Yourself**: While it's important to be open-minded, don't compromise your own values and boundaries. Be clear about what you're comfortable with and what you're looking for in a relationship. Authenticity is key to finding a compatible partner.

5. **Community and Support**: Seek out communities and support networks that align with your interests and values. There are numerous online and offline

communities for individuals exploring diverse relationships and orientations. Connecting with like-minded individuals can provide valuable guidance and companionship.

6. **Patience and Adaptability**: Understand that your journey may involve some learning and adjustment. Be patient with yourself and others as you navigate this new terrain. Dating after divorce is a process of self-discovery, and each experience contributes to your growth.

7. **Embrace the Adventure**: Dating in a world that celebrates diversity is an adventure filled with opportunities to broaden your horizons and learn more about yourself. Embrace the excitement of meeting people from all walks of life and be open to the unexpected.

At the end of the day it is up to you to decide what type of relationship you are looking for, go with what feels right for you!

Navigating Dating as a Member of the LGBTQ+ Community

One of the most important aspects of navigating the dating world as an LGBTQ+ individual is embracing your authentic self. Be proud of who you are and own your identity.

This confidence will attract like-minded individuals who appreciate and value you for who you truly are. Embracing your authenticity also helps in filtering out potential partners who may not be supportive or understanding of your identity. Remember that you deserve love and respect just as much as anyone else.

The first step is to give yourself time to heal and rediscover who you are outside of your past relationship. You might feel pressured to jump back into dating right away, but it's important to remember that there's no rush.

It's okay if you don't feel ready yet.

Just like everyone else, members of the LGBTQ+ community need time for self-reflection and self-love before diving back into the dating pool. It's also perfectly fine if you're excited and eager to meet new people; just confirm it comes from a place of wanting companionship rather than needing validation.

• Don't Rush To Go On Dates

The pressures and expectations can seem overwhelming, especially if you've been out of practice for a while. But one crucial piece of advice to remember is this: don't rush. Figure out the kinds of connections and relationships that you want to have.

If your previous relationship was in the closet, would you still wish to pursue that type of relationship in the future, or would you want one where you are both open about it?

What kind of partner would you like – pansexual, bisexual, or gay/lesbian? How would you wish to pursue the relationship – serious, casual, sexual only?

Give yourself the gift of time as you ease back into the world of dating. It's natural to experience the impulse to immediately dive into a new relationship, especially if your last one ended abruptly or unhappily.

Loneliness might creep in, and concerns about finding someone who genuinely comprehends and values you may surface. However, hurrying this process will likely result in errors and you run the potential of further heartache.

• Lay Out Your Expectations Early

Just because you are a community member does not mean you should settle for any less. When you start going out on dates, lay out your expectations to avoid wasting each other's time.

If you desire a long-term partnership, be upfront with it. If you want to date casually but with hopes of deeper connections, mention that. Laying out your expectations means disclosing your sexual preference to your potential date so that they are not blindsided once things get serious.

If you encounter someone through conventional means, and there are no immediate indications of their open acceptance of LGBTQ+ identities, consider disclosing your own queer identity early in your interactions. This allows them the opportunity to decide whether they wish to continue pursuing a connection with you.

However, it's advisable to assess the person's disposition beforehand. The aim is to protect yourself from potential harm or discrimination, so exercise caution when revealing your queer identity to ensure you are not unnecessarily vulnerable to someone who may respond with hostility.

- **Ensure The Date Is In A Public Space**

Now, let's address safety considerations when navigating LGBTQ+ dating platforms. Regrettably, some individuals exploit these platforms for malicious purposes, creating potentially unsafe environments for those earnestly seeking love or companionship.

Regardless of your sexual orientation you should always exercise caution when disclosing personal information online, not just personal or financial data but also intimate aspects of your life that could be misused in the future.

The dating world can be intimidating, especially when you're looking to meet people who share your sexual orientation or gender identity. However, it doesn't have to be overwhelming. The first step in navigating this new landscape is ensuring that you date in safe public spaces.

Dating in public spaces allows for both parties to feel secure and comfortable. This isn't just about physical safety; it's also about emotional comfort. In a public setting, there's less pressure and more room for casual conversation and connection-building.

One recommendation from a friend is to look for places where you'll not only feel physically safe but also accepted and at ease with expressing yourself freely. Consider local LGBTQ+ friendly cafes, bookshops or community centres as potential venues for your dates.

You can usually tell an LGBTQ+-friendly establishment in a few ways:

- ✓ Check if they have 'LGBTQ+ friendly' or 'Transgender Safe space' on their Google business listings
- ✓ Keep an eye out to see if they fly the rainbow flag
- ✓ Look for businesses owned by LGBTQ+ people
- ✓ Pay attention to venues that host pride events
- ✓ Take recommendations from your community or friends on social media

Aside from apps, consider joining a social group to meet someone in real life first and get to know them in a social way.

There are many great LGBTQ+ social groups that operate all over the world, Frontrunners is a perfect place to meet fellow LGBTQ+ people who share an interest in walking or running. Many cities worldwide have LGBTQ+ community centres that host events, support groups, and social gatherings.

- **Let Someone Close To You Know Your Whereabouts**

Prioritizing safety in the dating world is essential, and one effective practice is having a "safe call" protocol. Before heading out on a date, whether through an LGBTQ+ dating app or any other means, inform a trusted friend or family member about your plans.

"Always have a safe call," was the succinct word from my friend Peter.

Share details such as the location of your date, the name of the person you're meeting, and your expected return time. This precaution ensures that someone knows where you are and can check in on you if necessary.

It's a simple yet crucial step in fostering a sense of security while dating and can provide peace of mind for both you and your loved ones.

• Change Your Approach to Dating

One of the things I enjoy seeing most in queer relationships is seeing how the traditional norms of boy asks girl out have been flipped. In the LGBTQ+ dating scene, anyone makes the first move and people date people that they genuinely like and feel attracted to.

Let me share a story about my friend Peter, who discovered the intricacies of the LGBTQ+ dating world firsthand.

Peter, a gay man, found himself back in the dating game after a challenging divorce. Eager to explore his identity and connect with like-minded individuals, he ventured into the LGBTQ+ dating world. What he quickly realized was that after 10 years in a monogamous relationship –the LGBTQ+ community often embraced a more open and exploratory approach to relationships.

One evening, over a cup of coffee, Peter confided in me about his experiences. He shared that he'd met someone special named Alex, a charming and open-minded guy. However, Alex was candid from the start about his preference for open relationships, a concept Peter was initially unfamiliar with. Intrigued yet apprehensive, Peter decided to give it a try, acknowledging that love could take many forms.

As Peter embarked on this journey, he discovered that open relationships within the LGBTQ+ community often involved clear communication, trust, and a deep level of understanding between partners.

While it was an adjustment for him, Peter recognized the beauty in the freedom to explore connections with multiple people without compromising the integrity of his relationship with Alex.

Peter's story reminds us that the LGBTQ+ dating scene can potentially be more open to diverse relationship structures. It's a world where individuals have the autonomy to define their own love stories, whether they choose monogamy or embrace non-traditional dynamics.

The key is to approach it with an open heart, respect for your own boundaries, and a willingness to communicate openly with potential partners, just as Peter did on his path to love and self-discovery.

"The most important thing is to find someone who appreciates and loves you for who you are." – Tristan Brody

Chapter 9: Developing Intimacy and Connection

Divorce can be a challenging and emotionally draining experience that often leaves individuals feeling disconnected and distant from the idea of intimacy. I know for myself, the idea of being intimate with someone else was the very last thing on my mind when my partner left.

The end of a marriage can lead to a sense of loss and the need for healing, self-discovery, and personal growth. However, it's important to remember that the desire for intimacy and connection doesn't end with divorce; in fact, it can be a catalyst for rediscovery and rejuvenation.

Rediscovering Intimacy and Establishing Emotional Connections

After a breakup, you might be inclined to harden yourself and keep everyone at arm's length, treating everyone who shows any interest in you with a healthy level of suspicion.

I understand.

But if you wish to find love again you need to learn how to rediscover the art of establishing connections and building intimacy.

Here is how to go about it:

• **Let Go Of Your Fears**

One of my dearest friends, who, like me, had also recently come out of a long-term relationship, shared a profound insight with me.

She said, "The yearning for love can often clash with the memory of heartbreak." She was describing how difficult it had been for her to open herself up to love again after enduring the pain of a broken heart.

As we talked further, I offered my perspective;

The allure of romance is intrinsically tied to the vulnerability it entails. It's the realization that when you choose to expose your heart to the possibility of love and being loved, you also expose it to the potential for pain.

However, it's important to recognize that this vulnerability is an essential part of the beautiful tapestry of life. We should embrace it without fear or hesitation. When you wholeheartedly commit to love fearlessly, you open yourself up to one of the most incredible experiences life has to offer.

So, as you contemplate the prospect of dating and forming new connections, consider gradually lowering your defences and focusing on the positive outcomes you desire. The potential rewards of love should serve as a compelling reason to let go of your fears and dive headfirst into the realm of romance.

- **Be Engaged With The Person**

Engagement in a romantic relationship is not just about sharing moments or occupying the same physical space. It transcends the superficial and delves into the realm of emotional depth and intimacy. If you're looking to cultivate a profound connection with your partner, active engagement becomes an essential cornerstone of your dating journey.

Active engagement means being fully present in the relationship. It means going beyond the surface level of interactions and venturing into the depths of your partner's thoughts, feelings, and experiences. It involves genuine curiosity about their world, and a sincere desire to understand them on a profound level.

To actively engage with your partner, communication becomes your most potent tool. Engage in meaningful conversations that extend beyond daily routines and small talk.

Share your dreams, fears, and vulnerabilities, and encourage your partner to do the same. It's in these moments of vulnerability that the seeds of emotional intimacy are sown.

Active engagement entails active listening. Pay attention not just to the words your partner speaks but also to the emotions behind them. Validate their feelings and provide a safe space for them to express themselves without judgment. In return, allow yourself to be vulnerable too, as mutual openness fosters deeper connections.

- **Make Time To Do Things Together**

In today's fast-paced world, where time often feels like a fleeting resource, it's easy to overlook one of the most precious investments we can make – time spent nurturing our relationships. Yet, the importance of dedicating time to foster a healthy and fulfilling connection with our loved ones cannot be overstated.

Shared experiences play a pivotal role in building a relationship. Create memories together by embarking on adventures, pursuing shared hobbies, or simply spending quality time with one another.

It's in these moments of togetherness that the seeds of intimacy, trust, and understanding are sown and nurtured.

Whenever you are out in the world, how often do you find yourself getting all emotional and starry-eyed watching couples who seem so in love do things together?

It is often spell-binding, right?

Well, what you are witnessing is a couple who are building intimacy and deep emotional connections.

And I am not just talking about going on dates.

I am talking about participating in sports together, going on a road trip as you do activities like bird watching, taking scenic tours, and traveling together. These activities demand effort and collaboration from both partners.

- **Express appreciation and gratitude**

Many of us have it difficult when it comes to communicating our feelings. It is understandable.

But what I've learned is that emotional connection and intimacy with your partner will not simply happen.

In the intricate dance of love and partnership, the steps of appreciation and gratitude hold a special place. It's not just about occasional expressions of thanks, but the consistent acknowledgment of the beauty that resides within your partner's heart and actions.

When you make it a habit to recognize your partner's contributions and qualities, you breathe life into your relationship. Let them know that their efforts are seen and valued, that their strengths are admired, and that their positive qualities light up your world. In doing so, you create a safe haven of love and affirmation, where both partners can thrive and flourish.

This practice goes beyond words; it's the daily gestures of gratitude, the little surprise acts of kindness, the tender moments of connection that weave a tapestry of affection and trust. It's in these simple yet profound acts that love deepens, and emotional bonds strengthen.

As you express your appreciation and gratitude, you not only lift your partner's spirits but also reaffirm your commitment to nurturing a loving, enduring partnership. It's a beautiful cycle where love begets love, and gratitude begets more to be thankful for.

- **Create A Routine Together**

In a world where Hollywood has often portrayed relationships as a never-ending fireworks display of passion and grand gestures, it's important to acknowledge a fundamental truth: real-life partnerships are not always about the grandiose.

Instead, they find their strength and enduring beauty in the quiet, everyday routines that couples create together. These unremarkable moments, often overlooked, form the heartbeat of a thriving relationship.

While I'm not suggesting that long-term relationships should invite misery, you need to understand that as you and your date grow closer, the next step towards becoming even deeper emotionally is finding joy in the mundane[xvii].

Building deeper emotional bonds often starts with a sense of comfort and security within your relationship.

One way to cultivate intimacy is by settling into a routine together. However, it's crucial to discuss and *consciously* establish this routine, rather than simply falling into it out of habit.

Establishing a pattern creates a sense of predictability, reliance, and trust. When you and your partner wake up each morning, you know who will handle tasks like breakfast, lawn care, and dishwashing. Even in moments of comfortable silence, being around each other fosters a feeling of security and connection.

While this routine may seem uneventful, it's actually a representation of everyday life—the very essence of a long-term relationship.

Nonetheless, it's essential to periodically break away from this routine together. Daily habits provide a sense of stability, but if adhered to for too long, they can become monotonous.

So don't let the day-to-day routine lull you into a comfort zone where you merely check off tasks from a list. Instead, consider planning breaks from the routine, especially on weekends.

Embrace spontaneity by arranging weekend getaways, camping trips, visits to friends and family, and other adventures. These shared experiences keep your relationship dynamic and vibrant, ensuring that your love story continues to evolve.

Emotional connections and intimacy demand a deliberate approach to your interactions with and without your partner. Even as we emphasize the importance of this emotional connection, it's essential to acknowledge that romantic relationships rely on physical intimacy as well.

Nurturing Physical and Emotional Intimacy in New Relationships

Navigating the path of nurturing physical and emotional intimacy in a new relationship can indeed be challenging and even awkward. However, skipping this essential phase isn't an option if you aim for a lasting connection.

As I've mentioned before, healthy relationships are built on intentionality and active engagement. It's crucial for you and your partner to have open discussions about fostering both physical and emotional intimacy, rather than leaving it to chance or the unpredictable fluctuations of emotions.

Below are some deliberate ways for you and your partner to actively nurture both physical and emotional intimacy within your relationship:

- **Talk About Sex**

One of the highlights of my previous marriage was when my partner and I began discussing our sexual desires during the early stages of our relationship.

This open dialogue played a significant role in strengthening our emotional and intimate connection from the very beginning.

Since I've started dating again, I've continued this approach, and I believe it's something you should consider as well. Many couples avoid discussing their sexual preferences, which can hinder their understanding of each other's needs, desires and pleasures.

To foster a deeper connection with your new partner, it's essential to be open about your sexual fantasies, desires, and expectations.

This doesn't mean rushing into fulfilling every fantasy right away. Instead, it lays the foundation for a stronger physical connection each time you engage in intimacy because you both understand each other's needs and desires.

Engaging in conversations about your sexual fantasies not only enhances physical intimacy but also paves the way for emotional closeness as you share your most intimate desires with one another. It's a pathway to a more fulfilling and satisfying relationship.

- **Keep The Touch Going**

You understand that feeling all too well—the early stages of a deep and passionate love where you can't resist being close to your partner whenever they're around.

To foster conditions for further emotional connection and physical intimacy, I recommend that you and your partner incorporate these loving touches into your daily interactions:

Develop the habit of making physical contact whenever the opportunity arises. Whether you're strolling through the park, engaged in random conversations, or seated close together, seize those moments to hold your partner's hand, place your hand on their arm or lower back, or gently rub their face, hands, arms, or legs.

These subtle yet affectionate gestures help cultivate a deeper physical intimacy beyond the realm of sexual encounters. They also contribute significantly to creating a sense of comfort and familiarity with one another, which is paramount for building emotional intimacy.

These acts of physical affection serve as a reassurance to your partner that you're there for them, a silent declaration of "I am here." When your partner feels and knows that you are truly present for them, it allows them to lower their guard and connect with you on a deeper emotional level.

- **Make An Effort To Learn About Your Partner**

One of the most valuable insights I've gained in my journey came from observing an elderly couple who had been together for 57 years.

They shared their wisdom, saying, "We never stop conversing, learning about each other, and asking questions." The gentleman chuckled, admitting, "It's been 57 years, give or take, but my memory isn't what it used to be."

His wife chimed in, "We always treat each other like it's the first time."

Witnessing their enduring love was truly heart-warming and offered a profound lesson on establishing and maintaining social connections and intimacy.

The key to fostering emotional intimacy, I learned, lies in actively seeking to know your partner on a deep, personal level. Going beyond their sexual desires and understanding their innermost thoughts and feelings forms the emotional foundation of a relationship, elevating it beyond mere physicality.

By keeping the lines of communication open, you continue to strengthen this emotional connection as both of you evolve and change over time.

This enduring connection, cultivated through ongoing conversation and genuine curiosity about one another, enriches the bond between you and your partner, making it a truly meaningful and lasting partnership.

- **Tackle Problems Together**

If you share a close bond with your siblings, chances are that during your childhood, you frequently teamed up to tackle various challenges, am I right?

Whether it was supporting each other through bullying, studying together, or even helping one another sneak out for teenage escapades, solving problems as a team was a common theme.

This approach, of building intimacy through collaborative problem-solving, can be just as effective in romantic relationships. Embrace challenges as opportunities to strengthen your connection further. Always approach problem-solving as a joint effort, even when you may not initially see eye-to-eye on the solution.

There's a saying that goes, 'It's you and your partner versus the problem.'

In essence, you are a united team, and as you learn to navigate adversity together, trust in one another deepens. This, in turn, leads to increased vulnerability and ultimately enhances emotional and physical intimacy within your relationship.

- **Create Intellectual Intimacy Too**

Isn't it a beautiful experience when you and your partner share your thoughts, jokes, and reasoning with each other?

This exchange exemplifies intellectual intimacy, a profound connection that deepens your bond.

When you and your partner are on the same wavelength mentally, it paves the way for smoother experiences in all other forms of intimacy. Engaging in open and respectful discussions on various topics nurtures emotional intimacy, fostering an environment where both of you feel comfortable enough to be entirely yourselves.

This, in turn, positively impacts physical intimacy as you find common ground in your desires and preferences.

To nurture intellectual intimacy, cultivate curiosity about your partner's perspective. Embrace their ideas and opinions, even when they differ from your own.

If, and when, disagreements arise, handle them with respect, ensuring you don't inadvertently push your partner away.

Remember, relationships often encounter rough patches. These can manifest as negative emotions, insecurities, uncertainties about the future, financial challenges, or even decisions about where to live. As your relationship deepens, be prepared to address uncomfortable topics that impact your future both as a couple and as individuals.

Both physical and emotional intimacy are essential for sustaining a relationship, so make a deliberate effort to build and maintain them. Recognize that physical intimacy encompasses more than just satisfying sex—it involves various biological actions that make your partner feel seen and appreciated.

Emotional intimacy goes beyond verbal declarations of love; it's about sharing vulnerability, trust, and allowing your partner into the hidden corners of your life.

Only through cultivating deep emotional and physical intimacy can you and your partner unlock your full potential as compatible partners and embark on a journey to establish a lasting and meaningful connection.

Chapter 10: Creating a Lasting Connection

After embarking on numerous dates and meeting a mixture of weird and wonderful people, you've ultimately discovered your ideal match. Now, you're eager to take the next step: building a lasting connection with them. Rest assured, I have some practical guidelines to share.

First and foremost, it's essential to recognize that movies often misrepresent relationships. Contrary to what you might see on the big screen, a lasting connection with your partner is often strengthened when you are alike.

But what exactly do I mean by "alike"?

Recognizing Compatibility and Shared Values

Compatibility is a fundamental component of any serious long-term relationship. Compatibility refers to how much you and your partner have in common, how you complement each other, and how you get along.

Below are some ways to recognize whether you and your potential partner are compatible.

- **Positive Interactions**

When you first met your date, what way your interactions like?

Did they evoke a sense of familiarity, as if you had known each other in a previous life? Were your moments together enjoyable, leaving you both eager to spend more time in each other's company?

Do you find happiness in similar activities and engage in straightforward, smooth communication with minimal hiccups?

Such positive interactions serve as potent indicators of compatibility. They suggest that you and your potential partner share a substantial number of similarities, making you an excellent match.

It's important to note that compatibility doesn't imply unanimous agreement on every matter. Rather, it signifies a tendency to align on most matters, even when disagreements arise, maintaining mutual respect for differing viewpoints.

• Similar Values And Principles

Another pivotal aspect of compatibility revolves around sharing values and principles.

Take a moment to contemplate the deeper commonalities between you and your partner. Consider your perspectives on relationships, your approach to treating others, and your definitions of respect and boundaries.

When you and your partner find yourselves aligned in fundamental views on various aspects of life, it signifies a strong compatibility factor. For instance, consider the realm of religion. It's not unusual for individuals of different faiths to marry and lead fulfilling lives together. While they may not share identical beliefs on every matter, their shared worldview fosters harmony, even with a bit of compromise.

However, it's important to acknowledge that not every value needs to be in perfect alignment.

In cases where there are disparities, mutual respect for each other's viewpoints becomes paramount, unless, of course, a particular value is a non-negotiable deal-breaker for either of you. In such instances, it may signal a lack of compatibility.

- **Acceptance Of Each Other's Flaws**

Discovering your ideal partner involves recognizing that even their most significant flaw is but a minor facet within the masterpiece that is your partner.

It's easy to love and accept someone for their outstanding qualities, but true compatibility emerges when you observe how willing they are to embrace your imperfections, just as you do theirs.

Genuine compatibility is reflected in the complete acceptance of one another, warts and all. It's about seeing each other's humanity and choosing to cherish it.

As you spend more time together, you become pillars of support during moments of vulnerability, uplifting each other through life's inevitable trials and tribulations.

- **A Shared Sense Of Humour**

Do you and your partner share a similar sense of humor? If you and your partner not only love laughing your asses off but also find humor in similar things[xviii], it's a clear sign of compatibility.

A compatible partner should not only be funny but funny in a way that resonates with your sense of humour.

For instance, if someone finds amusement in the misfortunes of others while you don't, it could lead to disagreements. Likewise, if someone delights in sarcasm, but you find it perplexing, it may become a significant point of contention down the road.

Enjoying the same kind of humour and sharing similar comedic tastes is a strong indicator of compatibility. While compromises can be made, generally, you should share laughter over the same things.

- **Shared Long-Term Goals**

Wait what? Hold on a moment, have you and your partner discussed your shared visions for the future? Are your life goals, including financial aspirations, in sync?

If they are, you might have discovered your soul mate. Shared long-term goals are a powerful indicator of lasting compatibility.

At its core, this alignment encompasses what both of you envision for your relationship in the long haul. When you both share the desire for a committed, long-term partnership, it lays a strong foundation for compatibility.

However, it's crucial to delve deeper and ensure that your evolving relationship goals are also in harmony. For instance, do both of you desire to have children, or is there a discrepancy in this aspect? Disagreements on this matter can lead to significant discord.

Likewise, if one of you envisions a tranquil life in a village while the other longs for the vibrant city and its nightlife, this divergence could create tension.

While compromises can be reached, it's essential to have fundamental alignment in your relationship goals to cultivate lasting compatibility.

- **You Give Each Other Space**

Another sign of compatibility is the mutual enjoyment of allowing your partner to be their unique self.

Compatibility, in essence, entails respecting each other's individuality. While spending time together is enjoyable, it's equally important to grant each other personal space.

This includes permitting one another to pursue individual interests and hobbies. Both of you recognize and respect the other's desire to have moments of solitude or to relish life independently, even when you're not in each other's presence.

This mutual respect for individuality signifies a significant level of trust within the relationship. Demonstrating such confidence early on can strengthen your bond over time.

Conversely, if you find yourself wanting personal space while your potential partner tends to be overly clingy, it may be an indicator of incompatibility.

- **Physical Attraction**

Now, let's clarify—compatibility doesn't hinge solely on encountering someone exceptionally good-looking.

When we discuss physical attraction, it means that both you and your partner are genuinely drawn to each other on a physical level.

Many of us experience an initial physical attraction to someone upon first meeting, even if immediate physical involvement isn't the intention. This initial spark can serve as a foundation for getting to know each other better and kindling a future romantic connection.

However, it's important to note that physical attraction can evolve and grow over time, especially when you have many other commonalities. Don't hastily dismiss someone you get along with just because there isn't an immediate physical spark. Give it time to develop, but if it never materializes, don't be afraid to move on.

While physical attraction and chemistry are crucial components of a romantic relationship, they alone don't define compatibility.

It's essential not to overlook other compatibility indicators simply because you experience strong initial physical attraction. Compatibility remains the cornerstone of long-term relationships, so keep it in mind as you seek a partner for a lasting partnership.

As you discover your ideal match and establish your connection, lay the foundations for long-term success in your relationship.

Building a Strong Foundation for a Long-term, Fulfilling Relationship

Developing a solid foundation in your relationship is one of the best ways to ensure that you and your partner last for a long time, maybe even forever.

Throughout this book, we've explored a multitude of topics vital to building strong, lasting relationships. From the cornerstone of open and honest communication to the significance of sharing quality time, being actively involved in meaningful conversations, and setting and respecting boundaries, we've delved into the essential elements that contribute to a thriving partnership.

But as we near the conclusion of our exploration, there are a couple of additional ingredients I'd like to sprinkle in for good measure.

- **Spend Quality Time Together**

When we mention spending quality time together, we're not just referring to the initial stages of dating. It goes beyond those exciting first dates and extends into the realm of consistent effort and dedication to being in each other's company.

Value Each Moment! In the early stages of your relationship, make it a habit to cherish each moment together. Whether you're out in public or enjoying a quiet evening at home, actively value and appreciate each other's presence.

Those lingering glances from across the room and the desire to escape the crowd to be closer to one another are signs of a deep connection forming.

Investing time in building these habits early on sets a solid foundation for the relationship to thrive. The value you place on quality time together helps establish a positive and enduring dynamic in your partnership. From the very start of your relationship, make it a point to embrace quality time as a fundamental aspect of your connection.

- **Reflect and Learn**

It's essential to develop a habit of reflection, particularly in the early stages of a relationship. This involves looking back at your actions and assessing their impact on your partner.

Such introspection enables you to recognize when you may have unintentionally hurt your partner, allowing for sincere apologies and corrective measures.

The process of reflection also helps identify habits and actions that positively influence your partner. Armed with this knowledge, you can consistently nurture these aspects of your relationship.

While it is commonly recommended that couples strive to resolve their issues before bedtime, it's essential not to rush to conclusions solely because the clock dictates bedtime. It's perfectly acceptable for you and your partner to table an issue and sleep on it when an immediate resolution proves elusive.

This practice grants you the gift of time for further reflection and the discovery of optimal solutions, and also the opportunity to reflect and perhaps see your partners point of view wasn't so bad.

Throughout this journey of self-awareness and growth, remember the paramount importance of compatibility in your relationship. Finding a compatible partner is akin to discovering your tribe, your place of belonging in the world.

In the presence of compatibility, you experience a profound sense of acceptance and love. It's about relishing every moment, even when minor hiccups arise. It's a path toward inner peace, where life takes on a brighter hue. To attain this state, ensure that you and your partner lay a solid foundation for your relationship.

Be intentional in your approach during the early days of your relationship, for these initial steps set the trajectory for your future together.

Compatibility isn't something that evolves over time; it's established at the very outset. So, resist the urge to force compatibility with someone, even if a strong physical attraction initially draws you together.

Conclusion

As we conclude this journey through the intricate landscape of dating and relationships, it is only fitting to reflect upon the invaluable insights and wisdom that we've gathered along the way. From the initial stages of healing and reflection to the complexities of building unshakeable confidence and navigating the world of online dating, our exploration has been comprehensive and enriching.

We delved into the art of healing and reflection, emphasizing the importance of processing emotions and finding closure after a breakup. We discovered that healing is not just about moving on but also about finding growth opportunities in the midst of pain.

Our exploration included a profound understanding of building unshakeable confidence, focusing on boosting self-esteem and embracing self-love. We learned that true confidence emanates from within, and by stepping into our authentic selves, we become magnetic forces in the dating world.

The digital age of dating was dissected, where we learned to navigate the world of online dating effectively. From choosing the right dating app to crafting an appealing profile, we honed the skills necessary to stand out in the digital dating arena.

We addressed the common struggle of dating anxiety. We uncovered strategies to manage anxiety, cope with rejection, and avoid retreating into ourselves during moments of vulnerability.

In our journey, vulnerability and trust took center stage. We explored vulnerability as a strength in dating, paving the way for deeper connections. Building trust, both in ourselves and in others, became an essential aspect of our journey.

We became adept at recognizing red flags and nurturing healthy relationship dynamics. We discovered the importance of respecting ourselves and our partners, creating a foundation for thriving relationships.

The LGBTQ+ community found a voice in our exploration, as we navigated the unique challenges and joys of dating within diverse relationships and orientations.

Our journey was dedicated to developing intimacy and connection. We embraced the emotional depth of intimacy and learned how to nurture physical and emotional closeness in new relationships.

Our journey reached its climax, where we recognized compatibility and shared values as the bedrock of lasting connections. Building a strong foundation emerged as the key to a long-term, fulfilling relationship.

As we reflect upon this comprehensive journey, we understand that dating and relationships are not mere whims of fate. They are profound explorations of self, offering opportunities for growth, connection, and fulfilment. Whether you are embarking on a new chapter in your love life or seeking to enhance an existing relationship, the insights and tools you've gained are invaluable companions.

In closing, remember that love is not a destination but a journey—an ongoing exploration of self and others. Approach each step with openness, authenticity, and a deep sense of self-worth. Cherish the connections you forge, nurture them with care, and let your journey be guided by the wisdom you've acquired.

With heartfelt gratitude for accompanying us on this odyssey, we wish you boundless love, enduring connections, and a future filled with beautiful chapters of your own making.

Best of luck as you enter the dating world again!

Finding Love After a Breakup

Before you go

Please take a moment to share your thoughts and leave a review.

Your insights can guide other readers on their journey through these pages, and I truly appreciate your valuable input.

References

_____

i https://caldaclinic.com/dangers-of-suppressing-emotions/

ii https://www.psychologytoday.com/intl/blog/anxiety-another-name-for-pain/202112/you-have-to-feel-to-heal-emotional-awareness%3famp

iii https://www.bingedaily.in/article/how-dating-affects-your-self-esteem

iv https://news.arizona.edu/story/narrative-journaling-may-help-hearts-health-postdivorce

v https://news.osu.edu/study--body-posture-affects-confidence-in-your-own-thoughts/

vi https://www.ncbi.nlm.nih.gov/pmc/articles/PMC5351796/

vii https://www.psychologytoday.com/intl/blog/between-the-sheets/201903/why-authenticity-is-the-best-dating-strategy%3famp

viii www.tristanbrody.com

ix https://soulsalt.com/conversational-intelligence/

x https://www.indeed.com/career-advice/career-development/communication-styles

xi https://scopeblog.stanford.edu/2023/07/06/satisfaction-with-tinder-depends-on-what-youre-looking-for/

[xii] https://www.neurosciencenews.com/dating-apps-superficial-psychology-17980

[xiii] https://www.makeuseof.com/tag/online-dating-profile-picture-research/

[xiv] https://www.psychologytoday.com/intl/blog/experimentations/202207/how-we-communicate-affects-our-own-relationship-satisfaction%3famp

[xv] https://www.psychologytoday.com/intl/blog/happy-healthy-relationships/202203/the-importance-vulnerability-in-healthy-relationships%3famp

[xvi] https://repository.lsu.edu/gradschool_dissertations/1171/

[xvii] https://kalamazootherapygroup.com/why-routines-are-important-and-how-to-start-them/amp/

[xviii] https://news.ku.edu/2017/02/08/relationship-success-tied-not-joking-shared-sense-humor

Printed in Great Britain
by Amazon